W9-BUM-297

Adult Children
of
Divorce

How to Overcome the Legacy of

Your Parents' Breakup and

Enjoy Love, Trust, and Intimacy

Jeffrey Zimmerman, Ph.D.
Elizabeth S. Thayer, Ph.D.

New Harbinger Publications, Inc.

To the adult children of divorce.

Publisher's Note

This publication is designed to provide accurate and authoritative information in regard to the subject matter covered. It is sold with the understanding that the publisher is not engaged in rendering psychological, financial, legal, or other professional services. If expert assistance or counseling is needed, the services of a competent professional should be sought.

Distributed in Canada by Raincoast Books

Copyright © 2003 by Jeffrey Zimmerman and Elizabeth S. Thayer
New Harbinger Publications, Inc.
5674 Shattuck Avenue
Oakland, CA 94609

Cover design by Amy Shoup
Edited by Carole Honeychurch
Text design by Tracy Marie Carlson

ISBN 1-57224-336-8 Paperback

All Rights Reserved

Printed in the United States of America

New Harbinger Publications' Web site address: www.newharbinger.com

05   04   03

10   9   8   7   6   5   4   3   2   1

First printing

OVERTON MEMORIAL LIBRARY
HERITAGE CHRISTIAN UNIVERSITY
P.O. Box HCU
Florence, Alabama 35630

Contents

PART I
The Impact of Divorce

Chapter 1

PART II
Recovering from Divorce: Building New Relationship Skills

Acknowledgments

Thank you to the children of divorce, of all ages, who have helped enrich our understanding and have contributed in great measure to this work. Your openness and trust have been invaluable to helping others as we have learned from you. You have shared with us the dilemmas you face and the impact of divorce on your lives. The parents of divorce that we have worked with have also shown us their pain and contributed to our desire to increase the sensitivity of our culture and the system to the needs of the child of divorce. Our practice colleagues and staff deserve our thanks for their insights and labors as we all touch the lives of adults and children of divorce. We would also like to thank Catharine Sutker and her colleagues at New Harbinger Publications for their confidence in us and for all they have done to take the idea for this book and turn it into a reality. Finally, we thank our families (Laura, Jonathan, and Alison and Jack, John, and Rachel) for their support and love. Please know you all have made a contribution to this work for which we are so grateful.

Introduction

Divorce. Does the word trigger thoughts and feelings about caring, warmth, sadness, and compassion? Or, more likely, does it remind you of anger, conflict, hostility, and danger? The memories associated with your parents' divorce can affect your feelings about yourself and your feelings and fears about important relationships. These feelings can be quite intense, touching you at your very core.

This book is written for children of divorce who are now adults, who are sometimes called "adult children of divorce." It is written to help you look at the divorce and its impact and to help you take charge of your life and your key relationships. You do not have to feel continually victimized by the decisions and actions of your parents, which may have occurred long ago. You don't have to hold hostility toward your parents, hate yourself, or fear intimate relationships. It is not too late to heal the wounds. We've written this book to help you take back your life and live and love in healthy and fulfilling relationships.

As psychologists, we have spent much of our careers helping families cope with the devastation of divorce. We have seen the guilt, pain, anger, and depression of the children of divorce. We've been witness to the low self-esteem these children face. And we have seen the "children" as adults, trying to combat the long-lasting impact of their parents' divorce as, years later, they yearn for their own healthy relationships and try to feel good about themselves.

While most people pay attention to the divorcing family around the time of the divorce, few people pay attention to helping the adult whose parents divorced many years ago. Many concepts that are in place today to help divorcing families were probably not understood when your parents divorced. When we were thinking about writing this book, we realized that there are many books for divorcing spouses and for children whose parents are in the process of divorcing. There are also many books that include research about the negative outcomes of divorce. Yet, there are few books written especially for adults who experienced their parents' divorce during childhood.

This book is written to help you

- Understand major mistakes that parents and the system make when families divorce

- Recognize that you don't have to be a victim of your parents' decisions and actions

- Build concrete strategies to break the old patterns you developed as a child

- See that there may have been some positive outcomes to being a child of divorce

- Have hope and learn to have your own healthy adult relationships

- Learn how to effect positive change by taking control of your life

In *Adult Children of Divorce* we incorporate over forty years of combined experience working with children, adults, and families of divorce. We discuss some of the latest professional ideas about divorce and its impact that until recently were not well-known. We use actual case examples, short stories, or vignettes that have been modified to protect the confidentiality of the individuals and families to which they refer. In short, we have written this book for *you*, the adult, regardless of when your parents divorced, your own marital status, and whether or not you have ever been in counseling or read another self-help book.

How to Use This Book

In part 1 we discuss some of the reasons and factors involved in your parents' divorce having a long-lasting impact on you, even into adulthood. We examine why divorce can be so scary and difficult, the emotions children and parents experience, and the drama and trauma that may have impacted you as a child. We go on to talk about the impossible choices and stresses you may have faced if one or both of your parents also became involved in new relationships. This section builds a foundation for the work in part 2, and should be read before moving on.

The second part of the book is the "how to" segment. Here, we focus on how to take care of yourself emotionally, healing your relationships(s) with your parent(s), building other healthy relationships, building committed intimate relationships, and raising children in a healthy, loving adult environment.

Throughout the book you will find short exercises or surveys. You might find it useful to keep a small notebook handy to record your answers and thoughts. There are no right or wrong answers and no passing or failing grades. Instead, we are giving you the opportunity to look at and rethink old concepts.

We have also included short stories or vignettes in many of the chapters to help give you a sense of what other adult children of divorce have experienced. The situations and feelings they depict are based on actual situations that have occurred.

In some respects we view this book as a how-to manual for learning what you may not have fully experienced or learned in your childhood. This precious knowledge does not have to be lost forever. You're about to embark on a journey designed to help you feel better about yourself and better understand the choices you have in your relationships today. You may, along the way, face some uncomfortable truths, feelings, and realizations. But, in the end, we hope you will use this book to help you learn the skills necessary to help you move past your childhood experiences and wounds into a full and joyful adult life of your own making.

PART I

The Impact of Divorce

Chapter 1

What Happened to Me?

- "I was minding my own business when my parents came to me and told me they were getting divorced. My life has never been the same."

- "My parents divorced many years ago, yet it seems the war goes on. I'm still forced to choose who I'm going to see each time I go visit."

- "Relationships never work out. I don't think I can ever really entrust myself to someone else. They're just going to hurt me at some point."

- "I really don't respect one of my parents. It's a shame I was born to them. I know they can't help themselves for being who they are."

- "I'd do anything to make a relationship work. I give of myself to the limit, but it doesn't help. No one stays."

- "Why can't I be good enough? At home, at work, in my relationships, I just don't seem to have what it takes."

Do the above statements sound familiar to you? We've often heard sentiments like these from adult children of divorce as they come into counseling, troubled by issues that have been present in their lives for years. Fears about intimacy, commitment, making choices, and doing the wrong thing are common and expected as the children of divorce grow up and have families of their own. Adult children experience many reactions to their parents' divorce and subsequent relationship(s). Yet, the adult children are the forgotten ones, as our culture focuses on reducing the impact of the divorce on the divorcing parents and their young children. Unfortunately, the effects often linger on well into later years.

The dynamics faced by children of divorce do not end when you turn eighteen years old. In many families these dynamics continue well into adulthood. Some divorced families replay the divorce over and over again at holidays, special occasions, and even at routine times when the child (now grown) speaks of one parent in the presence of the other. These dynamics can take their toll on you as they continually exert their influence.

The tentacles of divorce may effect many of your life events and relationships. Even if you've worked hard to understand the impact of these life events in therapy and in open communication with your parents, siblings, and others, your experience of your parents' divorce can still seem to shape your decisions in all aspects of life. In part, this is due to the major influence of your family on your thoughts about yourself.

As a child you learned to see yourself and your relationships through your experiences, what you saw, and what you were told. To a great degree this comes from the messages that you received from your parents and other influential adults in your life. These messages may have been clear or subtle, healthy or unhealthy. They can last well into adulthood and impact how we live, love, and view ourselves. Beliefs you formed from these childhood messages stay with you and can seem to form the fiber of your being. Unless you challenge what feels to be so basic, you are left believing the illusions formed by these early learning experiences.

What Makes It Worse?

Divorce, even in the most healthy of families, is a major stressor on parents and their children. Understanding some of the common elements that can intensify the negative aspects of the experience is important.

Facing Countless Choices

For example, there are choices about where to live, how to show your parents you love them, how to spend your spare time, how to be loyal to one or the other parent, and what to say when one parent asks about the other. There also dilemmas about how much to show your feelings about stepparents in newly configured families.

As a child, you may have often been asked, "What do *you* want to do?" While this may have seemed like a good choice for the adults around you at the time, it could have been very stressful if you were faced with the reality that this choice was often not as simple as it was in your intact family. You probably couldn't freely make a decision as an individual because you were worried about how your decision would affect the two new, and now separate, parts of your world—Mom's part and Dad's. Any decision you made may have even reflected your loyalty to one or the other parent.

Often, we think of control coming from the ability to make a choice. We can control our automobile by being able to choose how quickly or slowly it moves. If this choice is taken away, we feel the car is out of control. We then experience heightened anxiety. In contrast, children of divorce can experience a loss of control when they have too many choices, as the choices often seem to carry with them negative consequences to one or the other parent. Did you face some of these difficult choices? Here are some examples:

- Should I do something with Mom, or will that make Dad miss me and feel bad?

- Should I make a choice that one parent doesn't like?

- Should I choose to do something with one parent that I know the other would disapprove of?

All of a sudden, the choice that may be easy for the child in an intact family becomes complicated for the child of divorce. This perception can cause children to feel responsible for the welfare of their parents and as if they or their parents lose regardless of the choice that is made. It's as if no matter how fast or slow the car is driven, you know you'll be in an accident and someone will get hurt.

★ *Jill's Choices*

Jill is a twenty-three-year-old woman whose parents divorced when she was twelve. It wasn't an easy divorce. Her mother was quickly remarried to a man who had three other daughters, and her father remained single. Jill did not have an easy time with the divorce and often felt caught in the middle between her parents. Yet many years had passed and she was now graduating from law school. Both her parents were going to travel about 450 miles to be with her at graduation.

Jill was now faced with a dilemma similar to when she was a child. Since the divorce, her parents had barely spoken to one another. She never saw them together in the same place. Holidays and vacations were still spent apart. Coming home to visit was a virtual scheduling nightmare, even all these years later. Now they were all coming to her graduation. Her mother and stepfather and their children were coming. Her father and paternal grandparents and aunt would also be joining in the celebration. She wanted to celebrate as a normal family. Instead, Jill labored over the graduation plans for weeks (even in the midst of final exams). Who would she be with and when? Should she make hotel reservations in the same convenient hotel or have her parents (and the entourage) stay in hotels that were miles apart? How would she structure meals and celebratory activities with each side of the family? Jill decided to schedule separate meals with each side of the family. Ultimately, she was more comfortable avoiding the issues and possibility of overt conflict between her parents and the others present by adopting a "separate but equal" doctrine.

But did Jill really truly avoid the conflict? Not really. In fact, she actually replayed the years of conflict and parental disengagement by replicating the dynamics she'd experienced as a child on her graduation weekend. She lost the joy of celebrating this special achievement and actually had to concentrate on making the weekend about her parents' divorce rather than about her own accomplishment. Her law school graduation became an exercise in making choices that would likely upset someone, including herself. Her graduation was a distant second to the anxiety about her parents' poor relationship and interactions with one another.

★

Threatening Certainty

Children see their family life in much the same way as did their parents when they decided to get married: "For better or for worse, for richer or for poorer, in sickness and in health, until death do us part." Generally, kids don't grow up believing that parents meant "maybe, maybe not." This idealized view of families is perpetuated on TV, in magazines, and throughout the media. As a child, you may have been certain that your parents loved each other and life would always stay the same. Or, you may have experienced your parents in conflict or outright war. Even if this was the case, you may have been painfully aware of the potential demise of the family, but still may have clung to the belief that an actual separation or divorce couldn't really happen to your family. You may have even believed that you could have some influence on the stability of your parents' marriage. You may have believed that you had the ability to repair the damaged foundation of your family, that if you were the perfect child, you could maintain the stability you needed.

Consistency and constancy are an essential basis of child rearing. When divorce occurs, it shakes the structure of a child's world, whatever the age. Divorce creates a host of uncertainties. How many of these did you experience?

- Where will I live?

- Where will I go to school?

- When will I see my mother and father, sisters, brothers, grandparents, aunts, and uncles?

- Will there be enough money?

- Will both of my parents have to work?

- Where will I be going during school vacation?

- Will my parents date and maybe remarry?

- Will I have new brothers and sisters that I hate?

- Will other kids make fun of me because my parents are divorced?

These are just some of the kinds of questions that you may have asked yourself in the wake of uncertainty that resulted when your parents decided to divorce. Many children also become worried about the structure of their lives and how to maintain relationships with both parents. Their future is not clear or predictable. It may be shaped by significant financial changes, by new child care arrangements, or even relocation. What once was mundane is now quite the opposite. It's all up for grabs as parents make new decisions with the help of strangers (such as lawyers, accountants, therapists, and romantic "friends") who are new to the family but who now have tremendous influence over your parents' lives and yours.

Perhaps uncertainty was one of the only things that was consistent back then. You may have experienced the wild ride of your parents' good and bad times. Was there a fight and then a wonderful period of return to family life and lots of trying to make amends? Or did you experience the presentation of a well-working family until D-Day launched you into another world that came out of the blue? In both of these circumstances, children are forced to acclimate to a new norm. The announcement of divorce rocks your family relationships and may later cause you to distrust your own judgment about the quality of relationships in your adult life.

Growing Up Too Fast

Children of divorce are often catapulted into a world full of adult issues and exposed to adult problems in a way that children in an intact family do not routinely experience. No matter how much your parents tried to protect you, you probably were quite familiar with adult conflict. Single, highly compromised parents may turn to their children for behavioral and emotional support, a dynamic that's often called "parentification." This role-reversal can rob children of parts of their childhood during which intimate involvement with adult issues of finance, relationships, work, and sexuality is usually kept at abeyance. Children sometimes even become the caretakers for their parents when the effects of divorce devastate their family and render a parent or both parents incapable of providing safety, protection, and care. For older children in a family this role can also extend to being the caretaker for younger siblings. Both of these positions ask children to skip over or forfeit some of the playfulness of their childhood for a quick trip to the adult world.

In a divorced family, children may be expected to contribute to the daily chores, care of the home, and other routine jobs. This isn't necessarily bad. If kept within a realistic realm appropriate for the child's developmental level, it can teach a sense of responsibility as a team member. On the other hand, unrealistically high expectations can be overwhelming at any age. The loss of the innocence and freedom of childhood may result in you feeling either an exaggerated sense of responsibility or the need to act out and avoid responsibility and commitment at all costs. Adult children of divorce can become the caretakers for all. They work hard and show a serious commitment to their work but may find it hard to find the right balance in their personal lives. They can become workaholics, overcommitted individuals, and stressed out as they try to do too much.

The opposite result can also occur in the adult child of divorce who resents the expectations of others. You may have had enough demands in childhood and need to break away from either the continued demands of your family of origin or stepfamily or from the new demands of your own family unit. You may not know how to move through stressful times without feeling like you're not good enough. Opportunities to act out provide welcome relief from life's trials and tribulations, especially if you are trying to regain some of the feelings missed during childhood and/or adolescence.

In both of these outcomes adult children of divorce may harbor resentment and anxiety. As children, they are at the mercy of parents who lacked the ability or energy to give them what they needed. You can imagine these children thinking that their parents should be able to "just do it"—but alas, they cannot. As adults, these children of divorce need to search hard for partners in their lives who understand their strengths but also can acknowledge their need to be in a relationship that is secure and one where they can really count on each other.

Parentification can also leave adult children feeling inadequate. The legacy of self-esteem issues can resurface at many different points throughout life. For example, job changes, marriage, having children, aging, and illness can all lead to acute self-esteem concerns, depression, or anxiety.

★ *Super Sally*

When Sally's parents divorced, her mother started a new life. She became a successful businesswoman, met someone new, and within a short time was remarried. She also kept the family home and most of the assets. Sally's father rented a modest condominium and led a rather nondescript life as a salesman for a local store. He was not very active in the community. As a teenager, Sally would go to her father's on Wednesdays and every other weekend. He would be lonely and depressed, and she would help him clean and would often cook his meals for the week with him so he wouldn't have to worry about them. Occasionally, he would take her shopping, and she would help him pick out his new clothes for work. Sally's father was kind and caring and always very appreciative of all she did for him. They would take long walks in the woods and talk for hours about anything. He was a soft, kind-hearted man.

Sally went to college and did quite well. She was bright and highly motivated, studying hard and excelling. Upon graduating, she went on to medical school. She became a pediatrician and worked in a children's hospital affiliated with a well-known medical school.

Sally rarely dated while in medical school. Her schedule was rigorous and she was devoted to her studies. However, while doing her residency she met a radiology technician named Mark who worked at the hospital. He was a gentle man who was, as she described, "always there for me." He would wait patiently for her to get off of her shift and never complained when she was paged for an emergency during their time together. Sally would say to her friends, "It doesn't matter that Mark has less schooling and makes less money. That's not what's important. You just don't understand what love is really all about." Sally married Mark around the time she started working at the children's hospital.

As the years passed, Sally and Mark had two children. Sally's career continued to progress, and she was very busy with patients, hospital politics, and her research into a rare childhood disease about which she was rapidly becoming an expert. Mark was always there to take care of the children. Sally would often speak of their marriage as one that was "enlightened" and not "bogged down by the usual male/female role stereotypes." Yet something was gnawing at her on the inside.

Sally gradually became more and more engrossed in her job and less and less involved in her marriage. Mark and she spent less time together as Sally dedicated her limited time at home to the children. Their social life consisted almost exclusively of hospital and other medical functions. Sally began to feel "empty" inside. She would look at Mark and wonder what she had ever seen in him. It felt like they were "miles apart." He was a nice man who cared about their children but someone she was unable to relate to in a meaningful way. She could not see growing old with him and was confused, burnt out at work, and depressed.

★

Did You Experience an Unhealthy Divorce?

Divorce can either be focused upon both the needs of the children and the needs of the parents or it can be about winning and losing. In unhealthy divorces, children suffer greatly even into adulthood from their parents' conflict. A healthy divorce allows the parents to heal and to continue to work together in the best interests of the children. An unhealthy divorce stays focused upon old issues, continually playing out the old marital conflicts over and over again. These conflicts and dynamics can repeatedly affect you, from then to now—especially if you had to listen to the anger, blame, guilt, and sadness repeatedly over the years.

Conflict Addiction

In unhealthy divorces parents are often addicted to conflict (Thayer and Zimmerman 2001). Were your divorcing parents so used to the hostile interactions, the derogatory remarks, the volatile exchanges, the innuendoes, and the condescending statements that they couldn't seem to give it up even years after the divorce? Some parents fight it out in court well beyond the final date of the divorce agreement with motion after motion. Conflict rather than good coparenting provides the link between these parents. In unhealthy divorces, children grow up in a difficult world. They are constantly caught in loyalty conflicts. They become the messengers for their parents' information exchanges and unwittingly carry poison message arrows that exacerbate the conflict and restart the match between two warring parents.

If your parents had an unhealthy divorce, you learned that conflict never stops and that choosing change does not allow one to go on with a new life. Did your parents behave like adolescents acting out rather than serve as models for conflict resolution? As adults, children of divorce from high-conflict families are well versed in how to fight ineffectively and are not skilled in how to negotiate relationships in a constructive manner. Adult children of divorce who are still caught up in their parents' conflict, cold war, or silence remain caught in the tug-of-war. You may still be asked to choose between your parents and so may your partner and your children. Do holidays and special events become a virtual nightmare while you try to please everyone, get everywhere, negotiate the land mines of communication, and still try to preserve your own family traditions and memories? Some adult children of divorce just give up trying and allow everyone to lose touch. Sometimes quiet and distance seem to be the best solutions to these adult children.

Devastated Parents

Another example of an unhealthy divorce occurs when one or both parents are significantly compromised by the resulting situation. This can be due to economic circumstances and/or the psychological effects of the divorce. Either way, children suffer the consequences if a parent cannot find a successful way to build and manage their new life. These parents find it hard to focus on their children and their needs after the divorce. Not only do these children lose the old concept of family through divorce, but they also lack chances to form new family units. They may be attended to physically, but their emotional needs can go unnoticed. Parents in these unhealthy divorces are often suffering themselves from depression or other related clinical conditions. They may be unable to see a hopeful future, have a weak support system, and lack the skills needed to restructure their lives in new ways. If you had a nonworking parent return to work for solely economic reasons, you may have experienced a resentful, exhausted, disorganized parent who was there but not there at the same time.

If parents remain wedded to the conflict that existed during the marriage and during the divorce, they spend enormous amounts of time and energy back in the old situation and not on their children's needs, fears, and dreams. If you grew up in this type of postdivorce family, you may have taken on the hopelessness of your parents. You may only see lose/lose situations and have difficulty deciphering the negative effects of a bad divorce in a bad relationship you're involved in as an adult. Your ability to trust your own judgment to qualitatively evaluate relationships may be seriously compromised, making it difficult to stay or go, say yes or no, or commit or not commit. Relationship-ambivalent adults stay very much on the periphery. Their significant others, spouses, and children suffer from the inability to ever really get to know them in an intimate way. Self-protection becomes a way of life, even more important than soulful connection. Intimacy is far too scary because the result has always been far too negative and painful for them in the past.

★ Carol Was Invisible

Carol was the youngest of her parents' four children. She grew up in a family where Mom stayed at home and Dad worked in the local factory. Dad often worked extra hours, as there was rarely enough money. Mom did her best to make ends meet and raise the four children. The house-hold was often chaotic, and when Dad was home there were lots of arguments between her parents. There was always work that didn't get done around the house.

Carol's sister Ellen was the oldest of the four children and out of the house when Carol was about eight years old. Carol's brothers were on the high school football team. Dad rarely missed a game, as he was very proud of their accomplishments. Carol loved to read and would lose herself for hours at a time reading anything she could get her hands on. She loved fictional adventure stories and would imagine herself as the main character far away on some exciting quest. Carol was a good child who excelled in school, but received little praise from her parents for her accomplishments. This was especially so from sixth grade forward, as her brothers were playing football and her parents began to argue more and more.

Carol's parents eventually had a very bitter divorce. They spent most of their savings on the divorce and often told Carol how awful the other parent was during and even years after the divorce. She could barely mention one of them to the other without it causing a problem.

Carol actually described herself as feeling "invisible" early on in her therapy. She said she felt that she didn't matter to anyone and couldn't understand why she was even born. She did not want to end her life, but felt that her life and existence had no meaning or value. Socially, she was quite isolated. She had had two boyfriends over the years who had mistreated her. She had almost no friends, didn't talk to her brothers, and only rarely spoke to her sister or her parents. She did well in her job as a research assistant at the local university and loved to go for long walks with her Labrador retriever.

★

Are There Really Healthy Divorces?

A healthy divorce seems like a strange juxtaposition of words. What in the world do we mean? In a healthy divorce, do you experience sadness and loss? Do you experience anger and resentment? Do you feel overburdened and lost? In a healthy divorce do you question yourself and your judgment? Yes, to all of the above! The difference is that, during and after the divorce, parents effectively balance their own needs with those of their children. Parents find ways out of their marriage that lead to new lives for themselves and their children, becoming good coparents by working cooperatively together for the sake of their children and, in the end, themselves.

Good coparents are those who can continue to communicate effectively and make decisions together in an efficient manner. They remain parenting partners in a business relationship dedicated to the job of raising their children in new family units. They don't try to function in a unilateral manner but seek to consult each other because they know that this is the best way to help their children negotiate life after divorce. They are a support system for each other and they control the system of extended family, friends, and others who may attempt to ignite the flames of the old conflict. They keep the world safe and quiet for their children, carrying the logistical burden of divorce to provide as seamless a life as possible for their children. They heal themselves so that they can help their children heal from the divorce.

Adult children of divorce who grow up in these healthy coparenting families see their parents behaving with integrity. When telling children about a divorce, many parents assure the children that the divorce is not their fault and that they will both continue parenting together, no matter what happens. Then, unfortunately, many parents do quite the opposite. Good coparents put their money where their mouth is. They do what they say—as hard as that may be. They understand that their children did not ask for the divorce and that the children are the ones who have to go back and forth and deal with each parent on a regular basis. They see that their children have to adapt to a situation that they may not have seen coming, and they know that their children need to love and be loved by both parents. They do not ask their children to choose. Adult children of these divorces have the best chance of swimming through the murky waters of postdivorce families. They, in fact, can understand that sometimes a difficult decision toward change can, in the end, be positive, and that they can learn to trust their own judgment and also learn from their parents how to forgive. If your parents' divorce had some of these healthy elements, you may have also learned the true meaning of real parental love. Your own ability to parent your own children will have been enhanced by the healthy behaviors of your divorced parents.

Will You Always Be a Divorce Victim?

The strong feelings caused by the divorce, the general experiences we described above, and all the rest of your own unique experiences can lead you to wonder

- How could they have ever gotten divorced?

- What were they thinking?

- Wasn't there another way?

- Couldn't they have worked things out?

- What if they had just tried harder?

- Why couldn't they forgive each other?

It's only normal to think that there must have been something that could have rescued your parents and yourself from the agony of the divorce. There must have been something someone could have done, right? It is easy to assume that because of the disruption, pain, and overall negative fallout, divorce was the wrong choice. Organized religion, the media, friends, and family often will echo this thought, saying, "It just shouldn't have happened." Yet, maybe there were actually some positive aspects to the divorce. Maybe you're not just a victim of what happened to you as a child. Maybe divorce was actually the best choice.

The controversy over whether or not divorce could possibly be the better choice continues to rage (Wallerstein, Lewis, and Blakeslee 2000 vs. Hetherington and Kelly 2002). Unfortunately, these opposing views have created additional conflicts for parents having to make these very difficult choices and for adult children of divorce as they reflect upon their lives many years later. As you think about your parents' divorce, notice if any of the elements below were actually addressed by their decision.

Safety

In highly volatile marriages where physical or verbal abuse is involved, divorce may offer protection, safety, and peace. The family no longer needs to live in a constant state of high alert. Children can start to get back to the business of being children and not be parentified. They can return their focus to their academic and social lives as long as their parents' recovery does not impede that process. As an adult, you may actually see the decision to divorce as a brave and necessary action born out of the need for self-preservation. This example may provide you the strength needed to make difficult decisions throughout your own life.

Better Family Relationships

Divorce can also lead to the creation of two new family units somewhat similar but very different than before. It can lead to the development of new and sometimes better relationships between your parents and between you and each parent. In traditional households where fathers may not have been hands-on parents, shared parenting plans can give them a renewed opportunity to parent in more direct ways. Children learn that they can feel safe and cared for by both parents. They learn adaptability through the transitions between homes and look to both parents to meet their needs when sick, hurt, hungry, tired, and so on. In the horrific possibility of the death of one parent, children can feel protected in the care of the other viable parent. Male children of divorce may be more capable of understanding the partnership of parenting and the importance of fathers being actively involved in the lives of their children. Female children of divorce may expect their male partners in life to be equal caretakers without having to be directed, cajoled, begged, bargained with, or pleaded into parenting (not "baby-sitting") their children. As adults, children of these divorces will hopefully model themselves after their parents and provide the same high standard of caretaking and shared responsibility in their own families.

Happier Parents

Parents who may have been compromised by the emotional turmoil of their marriage may find relief through choosing to divorce. After the initial period of adjustment, they may, in fact, be stronger and more resilient. Children can benefit from the presence of a whole parent who is not crippled by depression, anxiety, fear, loneliness, or low self-esteem. Hopefully this new parent is more independent, self-reliant, and able to express him- or herself freely. The healthy divorced parent feels more complete alone than together with their former partner. A renewed sense of energy and strength allows this parent to give more, play more, care more, and listen better to the needs of their children.

Children who have the chance to grow up in these healthy divorced families see that sometimes people need to make very difficult changes in their lives but that these changes can lead to positive development. They grow up not afraid of change but with an ability to embrace it instead. In *For Better or for Worse: Divorce Reconsidered* (2002), Mavis Hetherington and John Kelly found that female children of divorce may experience an added benefit from their maternal parent. These children learned how to be independent, capable, self-content women. They saw that they could rely upon themselves. Their female role models were *survivors* of divorce, not *victims* of its aftermath. It would then seem that their choice of male partners in life might be driven by their own sense of self-security and not by the need to be dependent upon males for financial or emotional self-worth. The choice of a partner who can love and take care of you is most healthy when it results from knowing deep down inside that you can solely face change and take care of yourself but that you don't have to do it alone.

Sibling and Family Bonds

Divorce can also be beneficial to the development of sibling and extended-family relationships. The bond between sisters and brothers can grow quite strong as they travel back and forth between homes, negotiating their new lives and relationships. No one knows better than a sibling the real truth of the pre- and postdivorce family. In an intact family, siblings often spend time separately with each parent. Families go about their lives dividing up responsibilities, taking one or more children together at a time, but rarely taking all at once. Many parenting plans keep siblings together during all of the parenting time with one parent or the other. Therefore, these siblings may spend more time together than they would have otherwise in their predivorce, intact family. They learn to rely upon each other, take care of each other, confide in each other, and need each other in a more intimate way than they ever did before. This added benefit of divorce may serve them well as adults when they may again need to rely upon each other for the adult needs of their lives, the lives of their partners, their children, and their adult parents and stepparents.

A Larger Family

Many children of divorce also form more intimate relationships with their extended-family members, such as grandparents, aunts, and uncles. In some cases, these individuals provide direct caretaking while parents return to work. At other times, the parent and child return to live with extended family for financial or emotional support. These families can feel more like the traditional extended-family units, where grandparents and others lived in close proximity and provided relief, help, support, and whatever else was needed. Day-to-day involvement in the lives of the children was the norm, not the exception. Children thrived from knowing that there were many significant adults in their lives who could and would care for them. As adults, children of divorce may have the luxury of knowing their extended family in ways that would never have been possible had their parents stayed together. They see that families stick together and help each other without question and without judgment. Of course, this is not true of all extended families of children of divorce. Some retain animosity, resent the intrusion into their lives, and blame their own children for the demise of the marriage. In other words, some extended families are too focused upon themselves to see or do what will be in the best interests of their grandchildren, nieces, nephews, and so on. If you were lucky enough to have the opposite experience, your whole life can benefit from the special chance to feel that you're part of a much larger family community. In turn, you can implement a similar type of relationship with your own divorced parents, knowing that your children will benefit greatly from more intimate involvement. Extended family and friends can be indispensable lifelines for the children of divorce. The added by-product of getting to know them can be a wonderful benefit of their parents' divorce.

The Stepparent Benefit

Lastly, another aspect of a healthy divorce can be the formation of a new stepfamily. Stepparents provide a new cohesiveness and perhaps a way out of the old conflicts. In a good divorce, stepparents can be part of the solution and not the problem. Good stepparents teach children about love, kindness, and discipline, but most importantly that there *are* successful marriages. The children in healthy stepfamilies come to realize that if their parents are happy and loved and feel worthwhile again, then maybe they can, too. For the adult child of divorce, this is a crucial lesson for the future. When parents learn to love and live with new people, their lives may be expanded in ways that would never have been possible had their family stayed intact. New stepparents sometimes bring new stepsiblings from their previous relationships and even from the union with the child's parent. This can lead to more complications, but it also can provide a new family unit with others who have experienced the losses and changes of divorce. This newly constituted family will not necessarily be the Brady Bunch, but it can become an affirmation of the positive value of change and renewed faith in relationships and the institution of marriage.

Self-Reliance

Lastly, children of divorce can themselves learn to be more self-reliant and independently capable. The packing, organizing, planning, thinking ahead, and self-management involved in shuttling between two households forces the child to develop a level of self-reliance that is often not necessary in an intact family. Homework, clothes, toys, and other belongings need to get back and forth regularly. Children of divorce have to figure out how to negotiate their dual world with efficiency and lots of advance preparation. These are important skills for children to develop in preparation for moving on to the demands of adult work and their own families. Children of divorce can grow up to be resilient adults who have a capacity to adapt to different worlds and negotiate their physical and social environments with greater ease. Some adult children of divorce have even traveled so far or so frequently that they are old pros at finding their way through airports, on highways, and so on. Their exposure can enhance their social development and their education. Adult children often complain that in the best of divorces, the going back and forth between homes was tiresome and cumbersome (Blau 1993). No one liked to pack up frequently nor did they like the partly nomadic existence. Yet, their ability to move between their parents, day care, extended family, stepfamilies, and others provides them with life skills that extend into their future work, married, social, and community lives.

In short, you don't have to view yourself as a victim to your parents' divorce. Unfortunately, the benefits you may feel are likely to be greatly outweighed by the stresses of your parents' divorce. These stresses may have been intensified if your parents didn't strive to attend to your needs and their joint role as parents as they ended their marriage.

Hope for the Future

The far-reaching effects of divorce on children as they become adults are still being uncovered. Amidst the controversy what emerges is that there is a wide range of adjustment for the children. The news is not all bad (Hetherington and Kelly 2002) as there are "protective factors" that researchers say can actually help children of divorce have healthy adult lives. The outcome for the children in each unique family unit is predictable only up to a point. In other words, there is room for many things to influence each adult child's story. It would be unfair to doom all adult children of divorce to worlds of despair and desperation when many find such healthy avenues to travel through their adult years.

If you are reading this book, perhaps many of the effects of your parents' divorce still remain and seem inhibiting and negative. Yet, the resources available today to parents and children are well beyond what existed twenty or thirty years ago. The focus on good coparenting provided by the legal system in many states goes a long way toward teaching parents and children how to divorce as successfully as possible. The advent of mediation, collaborative law, use of attorneys for the minor child (who advocate for what the child wants) and guardians *ad litem* (who advocate for what's in the best interests of the child) all provide vehicles through which parents can be advised about parenting after divorce. Many states have required parent-education classes, which provide excellent overviews to the myriad issues facing divorcing parents. In addition, private intervention programs (Thayer and Zimmerman 2001) have arisen to help families with more individualized needs or those with high-conflict parents where children may be at much more risk. Psychotherapists experienced in this area provide clinical expertise, guidance, and support to parents, stepparents, extended family, and children. Additionally, support groups abound offering a climate wherein divorced parents can find information, learn from others, and even socialize. Still, children of divorce need their own, special brand of interventions, and this book is a good place to start getting what you need.

The next chapters will provide a more in-depth picture of the main areas effecting adult children of divorce. While the legal aspects of divorce may be long settled, sometimes not without significant battles, you probably recognize that the emotional aspects of divorce can linger. The more parents and adult children of divorce recognize these potential risk factors and intervene, the less the chance that the suffering will continue. Much of the early literature on the effects of divorce would leave anyone feeling depressed and defeated. Let's rewrite the legacy and the future for you, the adult child of divorce.

Chapter 2

The Emotions of Divorce

Divorce is often described as a roller-coaster ride. The myriad emotions experienced by the adults as well as the children are often unpredictable. Feelings can vary moment to moment and certainly day to day. The emotions engendered by a divorce run the gamut from relief and quiet to intense anger and sadness. You had and have your own reactions, complicated by being along for the ride with parents who may have a hard time stabilizing their own reactivity. While the legal process was in full swing, the system also drove the experience in whatever direction and at whatever pace the court and lawyers decided. The emotions associated with divorce are often not under adequate control and tend to have a life of their own.

Let's try to list some of the feelings that are typical of divorcing adults and their children. See if you can identify which of these you remember and experienced in yourself or in your parents.

- *Anger:* including hostility, hatred, vindictiveness, aggression

- *Guilt:* including shame, self-blame

- *Fear:* including worry, panic, insecurity

- *Sadness:* including hurt, disappointment, loss, depression, grief

- *Loneliness:* including isolation, rejection, negativity, pessimism

- *Relief:* including calm, peacefulness

You may still be experiencing some of these same feelings in your adult life as a child of divorce. These emotions may be related to old issues that stem from the time that your parents ended their marriage rather than from only current events in your life.

Take a moment to read the list of words below. As you do so, pay attention to the feelings or emotions you immediately experience. You may even want to write your feelings (just a word or two) in your journal or on a sheet of paper.

Money	Intimacy
Choice	Disapproval
Trust	Separation
Loyalty	Lies

Were your emotions around these words reminiscent of those experienced during your parents' divorce? If so, similar words and concepts you experience in the present can trigger and intensify your emotions now. The emotions of divorce can leave such an indelible mark on children that, as adults, they have intense difficulty separating the emotional reactions linked to the past from present situations.

Parental Emotions

It's a good idea to take a look at the emotions of divorce in more detail. We believe it is first important to spend a moment understanding the parental response to divorce. This reaction likely contributed to your experience and understanding of both the divorce and yourself. Let's try to decipher the sources of these feelings as well as their behavioral counterparts and possible impact on you. These are large clues to your own psychological development and your own negotiation of relationships in your adult life. Adult children of divorce have lived through the turmoil and the subsequent struggles that their parents encountered, but they may have also lived through years of tremendous personal growth and positive self-reconstruction. Remember that emotions do not always have to take on a negative flavor. Divorce, like any phase of development, can be tumultuous—but the result can often be inspiring.

The Angry Cat Strikes Back

In the context of discussing divorce, anger is often the strongest and most readily associated emotion because divorce often arises out of marital strife and conflict. Sometimes anger is explosive, in the form of direct physical or verbal abuse, and sometimes anger is more passive, in the form of omission and disregard. Either way, the message is clear that relationships can be hurtful. Retaliation is usually the motive for most expressions of anger before and after the divorce. Each parent tries their best to slam the other with words, behaviors, legal letters, and court motions. The volatility can be quite high and is often inflamed by the divorce process itself.

Anger can be vindictive when it is aimed at hurting the other parent with little to no regard for its effect on the children who get caught in the cross fire. Parents who desperately need to "get back" at the other parent are exposing their children to models of uncontrolled expressions of hostility. They teach their children how to use words and actions to assault others, instead of heal. Unfortunately, children also quickly learn how to mimic these expressions of anger and often copy the same type of responses in their own interactions with parents or others. They get used to these more theatrical expressions of emotion and don't learn how to express themselves in a more constructive and assertive manner. The entire family gets caught up in the hostility, and children often have the mistaken assumption that they are responding appropriately by joining in the same level of volatility they experience from their parents' exchanges. The result for the adult child of divorce can be a quick trigger and an impulsive desire to strike back when hostility arises. Controlling anger has not been modeled to the child and therefore was not well learned. Self-protection is of the utmost importance and unregulated angry responses permeate disagreements without regard for the feelings of others. When anger strikes, the claws are out!

★ Steve's Anger

Steve grew up in a divorced family with five sons. He described his family as one that was busy and active. "You had to yell to be heard in my house," he said. "For example, we all ate dinner together. If you wanted something, you really had to speak up or it was gone. There was a constant hustle and bustle. Our parents loved us, but had to take control of the five of us that, from oldest to youngest, were nine years apart. Mom had her hands full as a single parent and was often yelling at one or most of us. If we were bad, she would even call Dad when he was at work and then watch out! Dad never hit us, but boy, we knew what was what with him. He was a big guy with a deep bellowing voice, and he wasn't afraid to use it. He and Mom kept fighting and blaming our behavior on each other, just like when they were married"

Steve was referred for anger-management training by the human-resources manager at his company after repeated complaints that the employees who reported to him were afraid of his anger. At the time of the first appointment Steve said, "I really don't know what the big deal is. I don't feel really angry. It's just the way I express myself. I think everyone is just too sensitive. I mean, sometimes work can be stressful, and you have to make a point to people. Otherwise they don't understand that you mean business."

How do you think Steve's adult behavior was shaped by his childhood experiences? Even his views of himself and how he relates to others seemed to mimic the experiences of his childhood. Unfortunately, he worked in a company that had a very different culture, so that when Steve was mildly miffed and vigorously expressing himself, others were very intimidated.

★

Should I or Shouldn't I Have?

That's the question! A divorce is rarely a sure thing. A couple doesn't get married expecting to divorce; nor do they have children expecting to raise them from two different homes. Most couples labor long and hard over the decision to divorce and are torn by the guilt over making this decision. When parents then see their children struggling over the parenting plan or their relationship with one or both parents, they are again faced with the guilt-inducing effects of their decision. This sense of guilt can even extend well beyond the childhood years. When parents see their adult children trying to cope with relationships fraught with ambivalence or conflict, they again may experience the guilt of creating a divorced family and not staying together for the sake of the children. A parent's sense of responsibility for the happiness of their children is a powerful force and can periodically reopen the question of whether or not they should have divorced. Guilt over a divorce can result for a number of reasons, all related to your parents' perceptions or beliefs (not to you, your actions, or inactions). See if one or more of these might have applied to your parents.

They believe they didn't try hard enough to save the marriage. These parents question whether or not they should have gone into therapy, have said or done any number of things requested by their ex-spouse, or wonder whether they should have gone on more couple's vacations or spent more time at home rather than at work.

They believe they didn't try soon enough to save the marriage. These parents question whether or not they should have listened earlier to the signs that their relationship may have been troubled. They wonder if they simply put their heads in the sand until it was too late.

They believe they weren't a good enough wife or husband. These parents question themselves. They worry that they did not act in ways that pleased their ex-spouse. Consequently, they may have self-esteem problems or suffer from depression.

They believe their behavior was responsible for the divorce. These parents may have traumatized the relationship with their own actions, including an affair, substance abuse, gambling or other financial assault, untreated mental illness, or even a job change or relocation.

Guilt can leave a parent quite compromised in their ability to cope with life postdivorce. Just when things are most complex and one needs additional strength and energy to move forward, guilt can sap that right out of even the strongest of individuals. Compromised parents can create stressed-out children. If your parents had trouble letting go of the guilt associated with their divorce, you may have felt overly burdened. Did you experience their ambivalence and wonder whether the divorce was such a good idea? Did you wonder, "If my parents told me that this was a better solution to their marital struggles, then why are they so upset with themselves and each other?"

Children often have one of two reactions to their parents' guilt. They can feel that they have the responsibility to parent their parents and take care of making them feel better, in which case their needs are often ignored in the process, eventually causing them to feel angry toward the guilty parent and reject them. This is especially exacerbated in high-conflict divorces where one parent perpetrates the guilt, and where the anger of the children is reinforced over and over again. Or the child may feel that they have to maintain some emotional distance from the guilty parent so that they can function without feeling overly responsible for the parent's welfare. This can lead to a polite but disconnected relationship with the parent (and in other key relationships as an adult). These children learn to hold their breath until they leave home one way or another. Children of guilty parents who divorce and do not find some way to successfully cope with their feelings find themselves in a quandary, even as adults. They can have a hard time determining how much responsibility to take for their own behavior. They may wonder, "Is it really my fault or does feeling guilty just give me an excuse to stay in the bad feelings and not go on with life in a progressive manner?" Everyone does things for which they feel guilty, but endless self-examination does not have to be a lasting legacy. Let us not forget that guilt can often keep one connected to old issues and the old family relationships. It's time to move on.

Worry, Worry, and More Worry

Another emotional reaction to divorce is anxiety, which can cause both cognitive and behavioral effects. Anxiety can manifest itself by obsessive worry. Divorces certainly create plenty to think about! If your parents were excessively anxious, they were also probably very adept at thinking about themselves, their children, their finances, where their lives were going, and where their lives had been. They may have chosen to worry about everything. If they did, then they were bound to stay awake most nights, become extremely exhausted, and probably not be much good to anyone, including you. Worry wears others out as well. Anxiety can be a toxic experience wherein parents convey their concerns to children and expose them to parental issues well beyond the child's years. Children need parents to solve their worries not to share them without restraint.

Lo and behold, these children of divorce can grow up believing that obsessive worry and anxiety are a way of life that provides protection from potential harm. They, too, can become worriers, lose sleep, and suffer from chronic anxiety, possibly resulting in numerous physical symptoms. If your parents were anxious, you may have learned from the best.

Realistically, there is a lot to be concerned about after a divorce. A new life is beginning, and with that may come a new home, new schools, new friends, a new or additional job, and surely a new schedule. Even the anticipation over seeing an ex-spouse can send a parent into panic attacks. Children need some degree of protection from adult concerns so they don't take on the worry as their own. In addition, anxiety depletes a parent's resources and drains them of some of their ability to parent in a nurturing and supportive fashion. If your parents were quite anxious, you may find that you see the world as a threatening, scary place where you're frequently on guard for what will go wrong next. This can lead to constant "what ifs" and difficulty being joyful in the moment.

The Veil of Sadness

Men and women usually don't get married with the idea that they will inevitably get divorced. They have their dreams, hopes, expectations, and wishes, and their heads are filled with pictures of the future and plans for a wonderful life. Those who come from intact families have even less of a notion that marriage could ever end by divorce. They don't think it will ever happen to them. Those who come from divorced families know differently. In the end, what is equalizing to both is that they experience a sense of profound loss when they recognize that their marriages and families as they know them are ending. That recognition leaves them with feelings of despair and depression. Sadness becomes a way of life, and all that surrounds them is reminiscent of what could have been but will not be.

Divorcing men and women often describe their feelings in much the same way as those suffering from clinical depression. They may experience a more severe depressive episode, which will require clinical intervention or medication. These parents cannot manage their reactions on their own and need much more than support from friends and family or even from organized divorce support groups. Others may experience more of a situationally based depression brought on by the end of their marriage and it's ensuing legal involvement and conflict. In other words, the symptoms of depression may be experienced along a continuum of severity. They also come and go over a long period of time. This is especially true for those individuals who are caught in complicated divorces and for those who are mired in the quicksand of high conflict. In these cases, the divorce never seems to be over. Even years after the divorce the retraumatization continues. Management of depressive symptoms is essential for the successful negotiation of a divorce, especially for parents. Depressed parents have a hard time fully caring for their children with spontaneity, smiles, and enthusiasm.

Signs of parental depression may include

- *Sad mood and teariness:* persistent or episodic

- *Decrease or increase in eating:* this may result in weight loss or gain

- *Poor self-care:* a decrease in the usual pattern of exercise, personal care, and so forth

- *Insomnia or hypersomnia:* sleeping not enough or all the time

- *Low motivation:* it's hard to gear up for a new way of life

- *Hopelessness:* the future is uncertain and dreams are hard to come by

- *Attention or concentration problems:* the mind wanders, focusing for long periods of time is hard, memory gaps occur, and processing is slower

- *Guilt or worthlessness:* self-blame abounds and it's hard to feel good about oneself

- *Drug and alcohol use:* these may increase significantly and to the point of becoming destructive to self, others, and relationships

- *Thoughts of ending one's life:* these may be fleeting or persistent

The above symptoms all fall within the wide range of feelings and behaviors experienced pre- or postdivorce. Support and interaction with individuals who have been through the process or who are going through it at the same time can be enormously reassuring. A sense of isolation for divorcing adults can lead to a worsening of these symptoms and make intervention that much more difficult and ineffective. Even though the divorce rate is still often quoted around the fiftieth percentile, these adults still often feel alone and different, which can contribute to the depression lasting for years beyond the divorce.

In short, parents going through a divorce are somewhat compromised and emotionally hungry during divorce and sometimes for long periods afterward. The amount of compromise is dependent upon a number of factors which can include

- *Support network:* Parents without adequate support have a hard time simply carrying out the requirements of single parenting. The logistics become too complicated, especially if there are a number of children to coordinate, and the children's schedules and daily lives suffer from the chaos. Homework is not done, tardiness abounds, bedtime and mealtimes are very irregular, and activities are missed.

- *Parental conflict:* When parental conflict is high, children of divorce have to suffer the consequences. Parents are too busy fighting, preparing for court, going to lawyers, going to court, talking with others about the fighting, and reacting to the other parent to be able to take care of their children in effective ways. Parents in high conflict are physically tired, angry, depressed, and too emotionally drained to be able to give their children all that they need during this tumultuous time. Many times parents are misled by the mistaken idea that they are fighting for their children but the fighting almost always takes away from their children instead.

- *Finances:* Parents who are left in financially insecure positions during and after a divorce face enormous struggles to make ends meet. Life may change dramatically from once comfortable surroundings, vacations, activities, and other amenities to a much more meager existence. Parents who did not work or didn't work full-time may be forced to go to work more so that they can support their families. This may leave children of divorce in day care or alone more. Whatever the situation, financial problems drastically change the lives of children of divorce and their parents. Again, cooperative coparenting and a good support network can help to alleviate some of this stress.

- *New relationships:* Parents who introduce new relationships too fast and too soon are also seriously compromising the successful adaptation of their children. New relationships may seem like they could be support systems, but for children they bring new challenges that are sometimes too difficult to integrate when their new divorced family units are not yet well solidified. New relationships may again ignite conflict between divorced parents, thus catching the children in the middle of old issues. Early new relationships may bring relief from loneliness and valuable self-esteem boosts to divorced parents, but they often leave children of divorce feeling as if they have lost their parent all over again.

Depression is a treatable condition. Psychotherapy and medication work to alleviate symptoms and reestablish a successful level of functioning. Unfortunately, some parents turn to drugs or alcohol to take care of the problem. Both genetic history and availability combine to make this an easy and familiar, but often very unhealthy, choice. Obviously, parents who abuse alcohol or drugs can become highly compromised and leave their children in a position where they must take on adult roles or are neglected, abused, or minimally parented. As adults, these children of divorce are just as genetically predisposed. They have grown up with the ravages of substance abuse and can often either select partners with similar characteristics or, when faced with difficulties, engage in the same behavior themselves. This parental legacy definitely needs professional intervention.

★ *Please Wake Up*

Cindy's parents divorced when she was ten years old. She can remember that her father had probably been depressed for years. She remembers that her mother was the major caretaker and when her parents got divorced her father just got worse. When she would go over to his house he would be kind and caring but his voice tone and energy level was clearly depleted. Cindy's older sister developed heart palpitations and shortness of breath, but her father denied noticing anything that would confirm her sister's condition.

Cindy spent every other weekend, Wednesdays, and Thursdays with her dad. He often went to bed early and slept late whenever he could. If she had anything scheduled during the time with her dad, she was always unsure if she would get there. She relied upon her mother to inform and follow up with her father on her plans and appointments. Unfortunately, this didn't always work. One weekend Cindy wasn't feeling well and had not felt very well since Thursday when she went to her dad's for five days in a row. Her mother had spoken with Cindy's dad about taking her to the doctor, but he didn't take her. Cindy also missed her tutoring appointment on Saturday because her father forgot and overslept. When her mother came to pick her up the next day, she took Cindy directly to the doctor and found that she had a severe case of bronchitis. Both her mother and the doctor felt that Cindy's father should have acted on the symptoms much earlier.

Cindy grew up not being able to count on her father to have the awareness and energy to care for her effectively and efficiently. It was all that he could do to care for himself. His depression severely compromised her relationship with him. The relationship with a depressed parent left Cindy with a strong will to care for herself and not rely on anyone, especially men. Her independence was fierce and her intolerance for others' passivity and neediness was high. She had vowed early on not to allow herself to fall through the cracks again.

★

The Quiet Is Deafening

After a divorce, the world can seem to change drastically, and one of these changes is that you're more alone. The house is quiet and sometimes children are not there for long periods of time. The usual din of a busy household is silenced periodically and there is no one with whom to interact. There is no one to talk to, to share your day with, to tell a funny joke to, or just to watch television with. The quiet can be very difficult for many and exacerbate a sense of loneliness.

Some parents deal with the loneliness by keeping busy—maybe too busy. They sign up for any and all activities and make sure that they are out as much as possible. Some people cope by working more. They may justify this by saying that they need the income or that they have to make up for the time that they took off to go to court or to take care of the children, but the real reason may be the deafening quiet of being alone.

Others may just retreat and not engage. They reject invitations and stay home. They say that they are not ready, but they are also afraid. The loneliness may feel comfortable after a while. It may be better than taking a risk on forming a new life. It usually takes an investment by others to move these people from their entrenched position at home and at work.

Some people increase their dependency upon their children, extended family, and close friends. They may burden the children with their loneliness. It may look like they are wonderfully involved parents because they never miss an event, a practice, or most anything that involves their children, but they really can't begin to think about forming a new life. You can imagine that one child can provide a certain amount of activity but families of two, three, or more children can keep a parent engaged almost all the time, even when they are not scheduled to be with the children. Extended family can also provide a convenient safety net for post-divorce loneliness. Those lucky enough to be living near family can also fill much quiet with the families of their siblings and maybe even aging parents.

There is so much to distract one from the quiet, but getting used to being alone is an important part of a divorce. Unfortunately, it's also a poorly anticipated part of the postdivorce process. For many reasons, people are not always comfortable with themselves and need others around to provide a distraction from this anxiety, the quiet, and the solitude.

Boy, Am I Glad That's Over

After the divorce, parents may actually experience a sense of relief that the marriage and the divorce process is finally over. This is especially true when parents are going through a more conflictual divorce involving litigation and intense disagreement. Some parents also feel that they and their children will be better off after the divorce and strive to draw the process to a conclusion as quickly as possible.

Some experience these parents as cold and unfeeling, but they may have started leaving their marriage a long time ago. The relationship may have been dying long before the divorce even got started, making the experience sort of like living with someone who is terminally ill. On the one hand, you are grateful for the moments that you have with them, but you may also be relieved when they pass away because the pain for them and the anticipation of the end for you is finally over. You are no longer where you were and can go on to where you need to be. The divorce, too, acts as an endpoint of a chapter in one's life and maybe a starting point for a new beginning.

Relief is a common feeling and should not create a sense of shame or confusion for divorcing individuals. It is perfectly reasonable and acceptable to feel relief along with sadness at the end of a marriage.

The Emotions of the Child

Of course, your parents' feelings were only one part of the emotional consequence of the divorce. The divorce also impacted *your* feelings. In fact, this set of emotional consequences can have the most long-lasting and profound impact on you, even as an adult. Some of these feelings may be different from those of your parents, while others may be quite similar.

The Mirror

As a child of divorce, you may go through the same feelings as your parents. You may even experience them more severely if your parents are compromised by their own emotional reactions. Identification of your own emotional trauma before or after the divorce is vitally important. You can best be helped if your symptoms are treated early and if you are educated about the range of feelings that the divorce process stirs up. But children often take their cues from their parents, and if your affected parent was too stalwart to go for help, you may have learned the wrong lesson. For example, you may have learned to hide your feelings and that you were on your own in resolving these and other issues. You may find yourself saying, "Why should I ask for help? It's not going to make a difference anyway." Or you may have learned that divorce is not only final and life changing but also insurmountable. Parents who recognize the interference of their own symptoms and find viable solutions for help give their children the opportunity for new hopes and dreams for a different future—maybe even a better one. Compromised parents can compromise children and leave them with little to no ability to negotiate their parents' divorce.

The Legacy of Loss

The end of your parents' marriage can be understood as analogous to death. It is the end of what was meant to be, the end of traditions as they once were, the end of cherished plans, and the end of the family unit as a whole. The reactions that a child experiences can be similar to those brought on by witnessing a dying relative or experiencing a traumatic end. One goes through all the same emotions as in any grieving process, including denial and disbelief, anger, sadness, and finally (but not always) acceptance.

Children who experience the loss of a parent or close loved one are exposed to the adult concept of loss much earlier than their peers. They are all too aware of the possibility of endings. They become familiar with issues and events that their friends of the same age cannot even fathom. They know about sickness, the suddenness of life's changes, and the harsh realities of the adult world. They are forced to grow up quickly, often taking on more adult roles and positions both within their family and sometimes with others in the outside world. They are catapulted into a new future and are forced to give up many of their old dreams and ideals. Their maturity is hastened and their exposure to the world of adults is far beyond what one would expect or certainly desire for them.

Children of divorce are not much different. They also are thrust into growing up too fast and too soon. They're faced with the loss of family dreams and hopes for the future. They have their own dreams shattered as well as those dreams told to them by their parents when they were still together. Their world is turned upside-down, and they need direction and guidance in putting the new puzzle of their family together. They are not protected from losing their idealism and their belief that parents can always make things better. No matter what, your parents simply couldn't change the world back to the way it was or the way it was supposed to be. They probably could not help but expose you to their own vulnerabilities and their inability to make the world all right again. Your parents probably knew that you would experience pain, which is not usually something that parents knowingly inflict upon their children. If your parents coped through avoidance and denial, they likely didn't allow you to express and resolve your very complex feelings. This means you may still be dealing with powerful feelings of loss today.

The Right Stuff

Children of divorce can learn a lot about expressing emotions from parents who try to handle their feelings the right way. No one expects parents to do this correctly 100 percent of the time, and neither do their children. After all, children see their parents react to many events in any number of ways, some far from perfect. On the other hand, parents can teach their children some wonderful lessons if they can express their feelings clearly but not in ways that feel overwhelming. Parents also need to understand the developmental level of their children so that information and emotion are conveyed in ways that are appropriate for the age level of that child. Too often, parents present information that is too detailed, too sophisticated, too theatrical, too unclear, or too hypothetical. If this was the case in your family, you may have been left with the confusion of trying to interpret what you heard, or you may have experienced unnecessary anxiety about potential situations that never came to fruition.

The range of emotions that parents experience during and after a divorce is important for children to see. Parents do their children a disservice if they don't let them see the normal range of feelings and give each child a chance to talk about why the feelings occur and how to manage them effectively. The silence about divorce can be deafening, causing children of divorce to be left believing that their feelings are wrong or are too much for their parents to handle. Later on, these children can have trouble expressing emotions appropriately to others in their own future relationships. On the other hand, parents who are able to share emotional reactions without needing the child to take care of them can provide an excellent impetus for parents and children of divorce to heal and move forward with their own lives in productive and effective ways. The recognition that most feelings fall well within the normal range and can be shared throughout the family can be truly comforting.

In summary, as a child of divorce, you may have been significantly affected by the emotional lives of your parents both before and after the divorce. You may have experienced the worst that your parents had to offer. As an adult, you can focus on the losses or you can gain strength and courage as you challenge faulty beliefs you developed as a child and then integrate the changes and the experiential learning you have acquired. If your parents represented the divorce as a horrific event that created devastating circumstances, then it's likely you still feel scared and unprotected. Yet, if your parents represented the divorce as a sad but necessary part of life and demonstrated that they could go on to successfully recover, you may have been given a great gift. Divorcing parents can teach their children to cope with difficult feelings and use them in constructive ways to make their lives better and happier. The right way teaches compassion, responsibility, fortitude, creativity, and caring. The other way delays the recovery of the family and leaves you stuck in the mire of their divorce. As an adult, it's possible and important for you to begin to lift yourself from the trap of these old emotions and create a life according to your terms. This new life can and should include committed and healthy relationships, even a long-lasting marriage. As a first step, you should know that it's okay to go ahead and feel. Divorce brings its own set of undeniable emotions. They cannot be avoided nor should they be an impediment to developing a positive future and positive relationships.

Chapter 3

Drama or Trauma?

Children discover their parents are getting divorced in many different fashions. Some children experience the surprise of the quiet ending of a marriage. They were relatively unaware of their parents' marital issues. In contrast, the news can hit like a summer thunderstorm—sudden and violent. These children were also unaware of their parents' problems until one day the word "divorce" is dropped, and from then on their parents are in battle. For other children, divorce is the natural conclusion to months or years of parental arguing and fighting. These children may actually reach the point of hoping their parents divorce just to stop the verbal (and at times physical) violence.

There are also many ways kids discover the details about the divorce and what it will mean for them. In some families the parents labor over how to tell the children. Together, they decide what will be said, by whom, and when this will occur. These parents generally are prepared to sit down together with the children and answer the questions they expect the children to ask. Answers to questions about where the children will live and how much time the children will spend with each parent as well as the many questions about "why" are predetermined by the parents to help prevent excessive anxiety caused by the unknown.

However, in other families the emotions of the child aren't showing up on the parents' radar because they're so caught up in their own negative emotions about their divorce. Their marital relationship has broken down, and they are not prepared to work together. In these cases, the children may find out about the divorce by hearing from one parent at a time. These children get different perspectives about the "why." They are left with many uncertainties and often hear too much of the blame and anger that one parent has towards the other.

The overwhelmingly strong feelings of parents can make some divorces even more emotionally dramatic than we might otherwise expect. Think about your parents' divorce for a moment.

- How aware were you of your parents' emotional upset?

- How much anger did you see?

- How much of their hurt were you exposed to?

- How often were you aware of the opinions your parents had of each other (especially when they were negative)?

- Did the negative opinions of one parent for the other get demonstrated by their actions toward one another?

- Were you aware of late child-support payments?

- Did you witness arguments?

In our practices, we've seen kids who have had to watch their parents get hauled away by the police when fights became violent. Some children have heard their father call their mother a "prostitute." Others heard from their mother how their father was not paying enough child support, which she said showed how little he cared for them. Some children hear that their parents have each scheduled the same weeks to be with them for summer vacation, leaving the children to choose who they would rather be with. Others listen as one parent gleefully recounts how they videotaped the other parent to use as evidence in their custody battle.

You can see how any of these would add a level of drama to an already incredibly intense and scary situation. In actuality, there seems to be no end to the amount of drama in a child's life due to divorce. As professionals in this field, we are constantly amazed at how, whenever we think we have heard the most dramatic story, there is always another to surpass it.

Moreover, the drama does not end just because Mom and Dad are legally divorced. It often continues. In fact, it still may not be over, even though now you're an adult. Parents fight over who will take their child to college. They decide to drive together in two cars and then have a major fight at the rest stop. A divorced parent threatens to boycott their child's wedding if the other parent's new spouse attends. Newly wed children of divorce are pressured by four sets of parents to spend Thanksgiving "at our house." A father and stepfather have a fistfight at the bar mitzvah of their grandson. Could the drama get more ridiculous? Absolutely!

Unfortunately, the drama can, and often does, last for years. It can lead to acutely traumatic events for the children or to more subtle trauma caused by years of chronic hostility and conflict.

Parental Conflict Addiction

As mentioned in chapter 1, some parents actually seem addicted to the conflict. They blame each other for the virtually constant arguing. They take little to no responsibility for their own actions when it comes to how they behave with regard to the other parent. They fight extensively over trivial matters. And, they often choose to fight and not communicate with one another, even when a fight isn't in the best interests of their children. We've seen parents leave their children at school by mistake and then take the time to argue that it was the other's fault rather than rushing to pick up the children. Other parents have forestalled taking their child to get medical or dental treatment to keep arguing over which doctor is better.

Conflict addiction is the term we use to refer to the behavior patterns demonstrated by parents who have what appears to be an uncontrollable need to engage in endless hostile interactions with one another. These parents may display some or most of the following behaviors with one another.

- Little to no positive or productive communication with one another

- Frequent arguing in the little time they do spend communicating

- Endless legal battles

- Exaggeration of trivial matters into major disputes

- Difficulty exchanging routine information with one another on a regular basis

- A poor ability to coordinate routine child-related activities with one another

- Frequent blaming of the other parent for their own hostile actions (for instance, "[Other parent] provoked me to act this way by their awful behavior.")

- Difficulty seeing the positive attributes of the other parent

- Not accepting or returning telephone calls from one another

- Difficulty respecting the child's love for and need to be loved by the other parent

As with most addictions, this pattern of behavior overrides the parents' normal habits. It causes them to have a marked difference between their behavior and their views of parenting and makes them act in a manner that is inconsistent with how they behave with other people or in other circumstances. The addiction distorts the clarity of their thinking and actions so that they often have a clouded view of what is truly in the best interests of their children.

What Fuels the Conflict?

There are a number of factors that contribute to parents "falling off the wagon" of taking care of their children together as parents. First, there are many emotional factors. Anger, betrayal and mistrust, disappointment, fear, and sadness all contribute to the impulse to fight and stay in conflict. Often, both parents' egos get in the way of letting go of the conflict as they say to themselves, "I'm not going to let him/her win this time." What they often fail to realize is that there really are no winners when parents are at war. Everyone loses, especially the children.

Yet parents continue to fight. Some parents fight well beyond the divorce. We have seen parents with over a hundred postdivorce motions. Other parents come to us with binders of legal documents that they've accumulated in the ten years following the divorce. The battle rages on as they hire new lawyers to help them fight the war. College tuitions are often spent on this addiction. Some parents are forced to declare bankruptcy as their legal bills consume their life savings. Did your parents continually look to have a judge rule in their favor? Yet, who ruled in your favor?

Similarly, the mental-health community stirs up the conflict. Therapists encourage their clients to stand strong against a domineering ex-spouse. They urge their clients to have little interaction with their ex and not to allow themselves to be victimized. How can this approach build the sense of partnership that is required to take care of the children in a collaborative fashion?

Finally, we can add the extended family to the mix. Here we have parents' support systems that from the start of the divorce rally around each parent. They support the parent as the victim to the unreasonableness and at times even "evilness" of the other parent. Imagine the bind that the child feels when seeing both extended families over a holiday. Within a matter of hours they can hear, "You know, what your father did just wasn't right. We know you love him, but you're really old enough to understand at this point." Then, the child can go to the other side's house (isn't it interesting that we call it "the other *side*"?) and hear from another relative who is just trying to be helpful, "You know, there are really two sides to every story. Since you're old enough to understand, you have to ask yourself why your father would have ever done what your mother says he did. If he actually did what she says, he must have had a very good reason. I don't want to say anything bad about your mom, but where do you think that reason would come from?" So, in a matter of a few hours, the child hears how awful both parents are. What a wonderful holiday! A time of love and a time to cherish the family is instead spent desecrating the image the child has of each of their parents.

In short, these systems seem to be biased away from the children and toward the wishes of the adults (even though many divorce professionals, judges, and extended family are dissatisfied with this). Everyone says they want to focus on the best interests of the child, but instead they often fuel the parental conflict that keeps parents from joining together to take care of their children. The conflict keeps parents focused on the end of their marriage and their relationship as spouses, rather than on the ongoing joint responsibilities they have as parents.

Assessing the Addiction

It is normal for parents to have some degree of conflict during, and at times after, a divorce. However, when there is conflict addiction, the amount of conflict gets out of hand. Journal Exercise 3.1 is a brief rating scale that you can complete in your journal. Rate how often the following occurred, to the best of your recollection. A 0 (zero) is almost never and a 5 (five) is almost always.

Journal Exercise 3.1

_____ My parents argued about me or my siblings and the schedule of when we were going to be with each parent.

_____ My parents were so busy fighting, they messed up on the simple things such as getting to an event of mine or making sure I got somewhere when they had to coordinate with one another.

_____ I was painfully aware of the bitterness or anger that my parents felt for one another.

_____ I heard my parents arguing, even after the divorce.

_____ I was able to manipulate one parent by telling them about something the other parent said, did, or allowed.

_____ I felt like it was my job to take care of one or both of my parents.

_____ The transitions where I went from one parent to the other took place at public places because my parents could not be trusted to stop fighting long enough to exchange me at their homes without witnesses.

_____ My parent(s) talked to me about their legal or financial issues so that they could justify the anger toward each other and blame the other for their economic woes.

_____ My parents rarely talked directly with each other. Instead, they exchanged e-mail, notes, and the like.

_____ My parents made unilateral decisions without consulting each other.

_____ Total the above. The closer your score is to 50, the more likely it is that your parents experienced conflict addiction.

The Impact of Conflict Addiction

If conflict addiction was present, it certainly impacted your parents (just like chronic gambling or alcoholism would). However, just as with other addictions, there is also an impact on the child. Children love both their parents but are caught in the cross fire and battle that occurs between them. They want the battle to stop. Sometimes it seems that one parent is primarily the culprit and the other the victim. Either way, the children want the two people they love to stop trying to hurt each other.

Children often feel that there must be something they can do to make it better. They often feel this way about the divorce in the first place. They may think, "If I'm good enough, maybe they won't get divorced." Or they may think, "If I get sick, maybe I can bring them back together." These thoughts can intensify in the high-conflict divorce as the children are no longer trying to just save a marriage—they are trying to save their parents from hurting one another.

Yet, just as children cannot keep a parent from gambling or drinking, they cannot keep their parents from being addicted to the conflict. If you tried and tried but failed, it's likely that you felt some level of responsibility or guilt for the problems of your parents. Some children feel this so strongly that they can become depressed and even suicidal as they think, "If I wasn't around, they wouldn't be fighting over me like this." This is not a rational thought, even though it is certainly easy to understand how a child could come to this conclusion. The responsibility lies with the parents to overcome their hostility to free their children from the conflict.

If your parents couldn't stop the conflict, you may be left with feelings of guilt, depression, and anxiety. You may find that you have a hair-trigger temper and that your relationships with others are tumultuous. If the conflict was severe and long-lasting you may even now be caught in one of the most severe traps of divorce, something called "parent alienation."

Parent Alienation

We don't get to pick our parents. Yet, most people find that in spite of our parents' faults, we love and care about them. However, in high-conflict divorces, children are often put in the position of feeling like they have a favored parent and, unfortunately, an unfavored parent. In fact, the differences and distinctions between your parents could have become so strong that you reached a point of rejecting one parent or the other. The extreme rejection of a parent by a child is called *parent alienation.* In parent alienation the parent that has been rejected is called the *alienated parent,* and the favored parent is called the *aligned parent.*

Parent alienation is a complex phenomenon that is only beginning to be better understood by the experts in the field. At first it was thought to have been akin to a plot that was perpetrated by the aligned parent on the child, in which the child was in essence brainwashed by the aligned parent to reject the alienated parent. However, more recently researchers have speculated that parent alienation is far more complicated (Kelly and Johnston 2001). In addition to the actions of the aligned parent, the alienated parent may have actually participated in some way to distance the child. The child may feel angry, hurt, or abandoned by the actions of the alienated parent, making it easier to be distanced from them. Second, the child may feel that the conflict between the two parents is far too difficult or intense to handle. The child may choose sides to avoid experiencing the conflict and watching their parents at war. "If I just stay at Mom's I don't have to watch my parents fight," is the sentiment expressed by some children.

It may be difficult to fully understand how parent alienation develops in a particular family, especially because the facts are often difficult to ascertain in an undistorted manner. However, it's not hard to see the impact on the children who have been caught up in this process.

The Impact of Parent Alienation

The impact of parent alienation can be quite intense and long lasting. It can carry on well into adulthood and affect other important relationships. Here are some of the effects that are commonly reported.

Intense Emotion

Divorce brings with it intense emotion. Yet, parent alienation can further heighten this emotion. Not only does the child of divorce have to deal with the loss, embarrassment, anger, and sadness of the breakup of the marriage, but when parent alienation is present, the child has to somehow find a way to cope with the strong emotion of being intensely angry at, disappointed in, and even openly hating the alienated parent. One child put it this way: "If my father was tied to a railroad track and the train was coming, I would tell the engineer to drive faster." These sentiments are not those we would have toward virtually anyone else. They are reserved for the alienated parent. At some level, it's remarkable that there can be so much negative emotion attached to someone whom the child claims to not love or care about. Who else would stimulate such intense negative emotion? In fact, one might wonder if so much emotion is present because of a deeper, unconscious, underlying love for that parent that cannot be openly recognized or expressed.

More Parentification

As there can be much bitterness directed toward the alienated parent, there can also be an equal amount of caretaking directed toward the aligned parent. Often the aligned parent is seen as the victim of the actions of the alienated parent. It can seem like the alienated parent's fault that the aligned parent has to, for example, be divorced and live in such meager surroundings, or be depressed, or have legal problems, and so on. Who can help this victimized aligned parent? You've got it—the child. If the child joins with the aligned parent, they may feel it's their job to support that parent against the alienated parent and to make the chosen parent feel better. The child may actually be thanked by that parent for trying to help and then hear more of the woes of that parent, which may further intensify the parentification. A teenager may get a job after school, giving Mom the money earned to help her pay her expenses. This is all because Dad has hurt her so badly in the divorce and hasn't given her enough money to live comfortably. In such cases, the aligned parent is often unwittingly contributing to the process by taking the role of a victim in response to the actions of the alienated parent. By the way, the aligned parent's role as a victim can last for years and years, well into your own adulthood.

Difficulty Developing Trusting Relationships

Significant interpersonal relationships are supposed to be safe. Yet, for the child caught in a parent alienation situation, such relationships can hardly be thought of as safe. If you were in such a situation you may have seen how one parent viciously hurt the other. You may have felt rejected by one parent and an inordinate amount of responsibility to take care of the other parent. Where was the safety? Where was the trust? We often develop an understanding of trusting relationships from our primary relationships as children. When these are distorted, we can easily have distorted views about relationships in general.

Part of the problem is that parent alienation is not something that is easily recognized in oneself. You might think of it as akin to being bigoted or prejudiced in that it seems normal, natural, or justifiable to that individual. Even now as an adult, if you have virtually no contact or positive feelings toward one parent, you may not see it as odd or damaging while still experiencing the void left behind by parent alienation.

★ *Tom's View of Relationships*

Tom is thirty-two years old, and his parents divorced when he was eleven. It was a bitter divorce that took three years to finalize. His parents then continued litigation even after his father remarried. Visitation was always an issue. Tom's father repeatedly explained how Tom's mother wanted to keep Tom from seeing his father. He told Tom that his mother left him with few assets after the divorce and how he had to work double shifts to make ends meet, not to mention paying his huge legal bills. Tom's mother denied all of this, saying that she loved Tom and only wanted what was best for him. She said she tried to fight for him during the divorce because she wanted to be able to raise her "little boy" and that children belong with their mothers. Yet, torn between the two, Tom grew to hate his mother for all she'd put his father through and how she tried to interfere in his relationship with his father.

As an adult, Tom has drifted from relationship to relationship. He enrolled in substance-abuse counseling after being convicted of driving under the influence. In describing his social history he said, "Who needs a long-term relationship? Women are all after the same thing. They just want to use you, have you show them a good time, and move on to someone else. I would never trust them. Relationships are all the same. They last for as long as each person gets what they want from the other, and as soon as the thrill is gone, it's over. You just can't trust women. Tell them your life story, and they'll tell their friends. Show them you're weak, and they'll eat you alive."

★

Relocation

Parents moving far away from one another is a different but major trauma for children of divorce. When your parents divorced, you adjusted to having two homes and not seeing both parents together. Perhaps you had to adjust to two new homes or going to a new school. You may have even adjusted to your parents' new relationships (you may remember their first new "friend"). All of this occurred while you were also going to school, growing up, and dealing with the regular demands of childhood. Then one day, one of your parents says to you that they have something "wonderful" to tell you. "We have the chance to move!" they say. There is a new job, a better home, a better school, more extended family, or some other reason that is undisputedly justifiable. They are enthusiastic and excited. What does this mean to you?

It can mean one or more of the following:

- My parents are getting ready to go to war again about where I'm going to live.

- I am going to have to adjust all over again to living somewhere else.

- I'm going to see one parent less often.

- I'm going to have to spend a lot more time in the car (or on an airplane) just to see one of my parents.

- One of my parents already tells me how much they miss me. What's going to happen now?

The parent often feels happy anticipating the move. How does the child feel? Anxiety, anger, and depression again can become intense as the saga of the divorce is replayed in the battle over relocation. Lawyers may be called in again. The child may even have to participate in a custody evaluation, yet again. Perhaps worst of all, the decision may not be finalized for six to twelve months or more as the parents pursue legal actions and remedies.

Finally, the relocation occurs. If you went through a relocation, your life changed dramatically. You spent more time traveling from one parent to the other. You spent less time with one parent. You had less regular contact between you and your parents as you were with one or the other for more time at once. Some children in long-distance relocations spend the school year with one parent and summers with the other. You had two sets of friends. You had parallel lives in two different towns or two different states. You felt like you did not belong in one or both places. Once again, it might have felt like you were losing one parent, or even like you were losing control of your home life (just after things began to settle down).

In short, relocation can be a major disruption that contributes to the unsettling feeling that the world is not a safe place and that all the promises you were told (for example, around the divorce) just cannot be trusted. Life did not get better. You were not going to have just as much time with both parents. You didn't just have two houses that you could go back and forth between. Mom and Dad were not at all finished with the battles and hurt of the divorce.

Moving Closer

At times, parents actually relocate to be closer together. This can certainly be a reunifying experience for the child who has parents who have geographically been quite a distance from one another and now are in the same town. You can again have one set of friends, play on the same soccer team that your school friends play on, and see Mom and Dad more frequently.

Unfortunately, if not handled well, moving closer can be another opportunity for the child to get caught in the conflict of the parents. In a high-conflict divorce there are times when the geographic distance between the parents means little contact and little time for conflict. When one parent moves closer, it can feel to the resident parent that the other is encroaching on "their" territory. The parenting schedule battle can be ignited anew as the parent who had been more distant now can see you more often. You may have won a trip back to the custody evaluator's office to have someone sort out who you're going to be with and when. It can seem like the decisions of your parents continue to complicate your life and replay the divorce over and over again.

★ Rootless

Mary was eight years old when her parents divorced. Her brother was six. Part of the reason for the divorce was that Mary's father, a lawyer, decided to take a job out of state. The expectation was that Mary and her brother and mother would follow after the summer. That never happened and her mother filed for divorce within one month of the father's departure. Then, the long-distance commuting began.

Mary's parents routinely argued about the parenting plan, custody, and just about everything that had to do with the schedule. Mary and her brother saw their father every other weekend and for most school vacations. In the summer, they went to his house for a month at a time. The drive was about four to five hours one-way. Mary hated that drive. Her Dad tried to make the ride less tedious, but it hardly ever was. Sometimes their father would come to see them and stay at a hotel near their mother's home. On "Daddy weekends," Mary's parents usually met about one hour away from her mother's home and exchanged the kids on both Friday and Sunday evenings.

Mary was always tired. Most of all, she couldn't really sign up for activities in her hometown, go to her friends' birthday parties, or just hang out after school on those weekends that she was going to see her Dad. Dad's schedule was very structured and planned, so there was little room for changes to accommodate Mary's plans. As she got older, Mary began to refuse to go to her father's because it interfered with her studying, sports, and dating. She missed her father very much, but she felt that her parents' conflict and unwillingness to find a viable solution for her gave her no choice.

As an adult, Mary became quite a homebody and developed anxiety about going too far from her residence. Most of all, she had difficulty forming lasting relationships with others, especially men, for fear that they would leave. She frequently was the one to end relationships before she could get left.

When Mary married, she settled in to make a home for herself for life. She was a stay-at-home mom, volunteered at school, and was always participating in community events. Her home was impeccable. When Mary's husband lost his job and had to look for work in other communities, let alone other states, she fell into a significant depression requiring medication and psychotherapy. The family had to move to accommodate her husband's new position, but Mary had a very difficult time relocating to her new home and community.

Can you see how Mary's childhood experience during her parents' divorce framed her perception of a home and a family? Her own lack of secure roots left her feeling disconnected and unsettled, so that she was desperate for a stable home environment. The way her parents structured the relocation left her unable to cope with the normal events of the new job and move that her husband's career required.

★

Other Divorce Dramas

These are the day-to-day experiences that leave their mark on children into adulthood. As you read the next two vignettes, think about the long-term impact of these events on the children. How did these children feel at the time? How did these events affect these children as adults? How would you have felt if you were one of these children and you had experienced a similar set of circumstances?

★ *Frank's Lunchtime Surprise*

Frank was in fifth grade. His parents had been separated for about a year and lived about forty-five minutes apart. On Monday, after spending the weekend with his father he sat down to lunch with the usual group of guys. His father always packed a good lunch and boy was he hungry. His friends were all around as he eagerly reached into his backpack and pulled out his lunch. At just that moment, his underwear flew out onto the table! That's right, his underwear, right there on the cafeteria table. His friends had hours of fun embarrassing him for years with clever comments about not wanting to share lunch and then saying to girls he liked that they should be careful because of the special "supplies" Frank carried in his backpack. Frank couldn't believe, looking back on it, that his father was so compelled to return his underwear to his mother that he put it in Frank's backpack.

★

★ *Twenty Questions*

One day Lisa (who was nine years old) was at her mother's and a woman she didn't know came to visit. She said she wanted to talk to her and ask her some questions about her parents and their divorce. Lisa's mother said she should be very honest and tell her everything and she should tell her all about her feelings. Lisa's mother went into her bedroom and closed the door. The woman and Lisa spoke for a while, and she showed the woman her room. As they talked, the woman asked about Lisa's parents and how close she was to each of them. Lisa told her how she and her father loved to tickle each other. Lisa told her that when she visited her father, they would snuggle at night in bed until she fell asleep, sometimes in her bed and sometimes in his. Lisa and the woman talked for a while more, and then she left. After that, things were never the same. Lisa saw her father much less often and when she did, they had to visit in a special divorce center with a one-way mirror. Lisa's father was always nice, but seemed very sad and was not affectionate after that time. Only later when she was older did Lisa realize that her mother had her talk to someone from child protective services. That person then decided that Lisa had to have supervised visitation with her father. Lisa couldn't believe she did that. But what's worse, Lisa couldn't believe that she caused her father that kind of pain. All he did was love her. Lisa said something that took her away from him. She felt like an idiot, and like she had been duped.

★

Other Traumas and Losses

While the divorce and its surrounding problems can seem like the most stressful events, life still goes on and can manage to dish out other stresses and traumas along the way. Relatives, friends, and even pets may get sick and die. Other people who are close to you leave in other ways. There are social disappointments, unfair teachers, and friends who always leave you out. You may have had your own serious illnesses or very stressful life events or abuse or trauma from other sources. All of this can further replay the dynamics of the divorce as you seek support from your parents.

In a healthy family system, parents support the child. The child feels parental love and caring and has a sense of their parents' emotional strength. When there are bumps in the road, there may be a sense or attitude of "we can and we will get through this together." This can happen in a divorced family as well. In one particular family, the child's grandparent was dying. Both parents strategized a plan for how they would tell the child. The parents lived over three hours away from one another, yet they were able to recognize that the grandparent's death was a major loss for their child. It didn't matter whether it was Mom's or Dad's parent that died. What mattered was that their child was experiencing a painful loss and they wanted to comfort her as best as possible. They were, in fact, able to do just that without power struggles or excess stress.

In unhealthy family systems the loss can take on a life of its own. If you had trauma and loss as a child, think back and ask yourself these questions.

- Did my parents make the loss *their* problem? Was it about them or about me?

- Did I somehow feel blamed for the loss or trauma?

- Did I feel like I was being selfish when I was upset about the situation?

- Did my parents get into an arguments about the situation?

- Was I comforted enough by my parents?

- Did my parents work together to see to it that I got what I needed?

If you answered yes to the first four questions and no to the last two questions you may have been in a family situation where there was high conflict and where your parents consequently had difficulty focusing on you, the child. It is not that you weren't loved or important. It is that their issues and addiction to the conflict distorted their focus, making it much harder for them to pay attention to your needs.

In short, the drama and the trauma may have taught you that the world is a scary place and that the family is not a place you can depend on to feel comforted and protected. Instead of seeing parents stand together to protect you, you may have seen them attack one another. This is powerful learning, yet it only relates to one family system—the one in which you grew up. What is so hard to remember is that the sum total of your experiences about families and significant relationships as a child primarily comes from the one experience of your own family. Many children growing up in conflict-addicted or otherwise compromised families don't want to take the risk to allow themselves to be vulnerable to more pain. The losses suffered are just too great, and they do not believe their own adult relationships can work in ways that are long-lasting, safe, and fulfilling. But reading and working through the material in this book can be your first step toward realizing that you *can* build a strong, healthy life and love—and that you deserve to.

Chapter 4

Loyalty Conflicts: How Can You Choose?

When your parents divorced, their support systems rallied around them and helped them make the countless choices facing them. How would the money be split up? Where would they live? Who would get what pieces of furniture? They even had help deciding where you would be and when. While some of these decisions may have been difficult and heart wrenching, they had friends and family and, of course, attorneys in their corner supporting them through the process of divorce.

Unfortunately, few people pay attention to the choices that confront the children involved. Some of these choices are outright impossible for kids to make. Others are more subtle choices that still shouldn't be made by children. Either way, these choices put children in difficult positions that cause them to experience feelings such as anxiety and anger that are similar to those of their parents (as we discussed in chapter 2). We'll explore more about these feelings in the second part of this chapter.

Below are some actual choices that children have been asked to make. As you read them, see how similar they are to some of your own experiences. What are the elements of these situations that make these choices so difficult?

- "I was the younger of two children. The judge talked to my sister first and asked her who she wanted to live with. She chose our father. The judge then turned to me and asked me the same question. I wanted to go with my father, but felt I had to pick my mother."

- A parent says to the child, "Listen, this will be our secret. No matter what, don't tell your mom about my friend staying over last night. It will just get her upset for no reason."

- "They asked me if I'd like to continue to go to school with my friends and live with Dad or go to a new school and live with Mom."

- "At the end of my concert, my mom and dad were on different sides of the auditorium. Should I go to Mom first, or should I go to Dad since it's his night?"

You can see that making choices such as these can make children feel pulled between their parents. The children will lose either way, even though they are the ones who hold the decision cards. This is far too much for any child to handle.

Journal Exercise 4.1

Think about some of the choices that challenged your feelings of loyalty toward one or both parents during or after their divorce. What were the three most difficult ones that come to mind? Write your answers in your journal.

1.

2.

3.

As you think about these choices, consider how they differ from many other choices you have made in life. Most choices give us a sense of control. By making most decisions, we determine our fate—or at least it sometimes seems that way. We can decide what to wear, what kind of job to take, who we will date or marry, what kind of car to drive, what to eat, and so on. Wars have been fought to preserve basic freedoms of choice. When the freedom to choose is taken away from us, we often feel depressed, angry, or anxious.

At times, the choices we face can be difficult. We may have competing needs or values.

- Should I work or go out with my friends?

- Should I drive faster or take longer to get where I'm going?

- Should I pass up the chocolate cake or not?

- Should I go on vacation or save money for retirement?

These kinds of choices often lead to a sense of internal conflict. We may struggle with them and even feel guilty about the choices we make. We look to our values and determine the pros and cons around the different options. We get information and advice in the hope of making a more informed decision. We often wrestle with relatively simple decisions. However, most of the time the choices before us are not ones that will hurt the people we love.

In divorce, this is different—very different. The choices that are put before children do not lead to a sense of control. Rather, they often lead to the child being placed in a position of feeling like they are betraying one parent or the other (or both). In essence, the child is put in a position where their actions are going to hurt (or seem to hurt) one or both of the people they love the most. It's like asking a parent to decide which child should not eat tonight or which child should get hurt or sick. We would look at these choices as impossible ones for a parent to make. Yet, parents and the system have asked children of divorce to make these types of decisions for years. How many of the decisions that you listed in Journal Exercise 4.1 were decisions where one or both parents would be affected? Children of divorce are often presented with decisions that are not theirs to make. Unfortunately, they are often asked for input on decisions that will negatively impact one or both parents. They are, in essence, forced to try to decide with which parent their loyalty lies.

Types of Choices

One way of starting to sort this out is to look at the some of the common types of choices that you may have been asked to make. We have found that many choices can fit into some of these categories.

Time with Each Parent

- Where do I live?

- When am I with each parent?

- Should I stay over the weekend with the parent who just grounded me?

- Where should I go to school?

- Should I go to my friend's party or stay at home with the parent I see less often?

Parental Worth

- Which parent is the warmest?

- Which parent is the best cook?

- Which parent takes care of me the best?

- Which parent do I hug first when they are both at the school play?

- Which parent is a better person?

- Which parent gives me more freedom?

- Which parent disciplines me less?

- Who do I talk to about important personal problems?

- Who do I ask for something I want or need?

- Who can I talk to about my feelings?

Protecting Parents' Emotions

- Do I tell one parent I had a good time with the other?

- Do I tell one parent the other has a new "friend" who is really nice?

- Do I tell one parent the other just bought a new car or is moving to an expensive home?

- Do I ask one parent to take me back early to the other parent?

Loyalty: The Most Difficult Choice

The choices above have many different psychological components. Yet, those that may have forced you to confront the loyalty you had for one parent or the other are likely to be the most difficult. Some of these choices may have led you to one or more of the following dilemmas.

Keeping Secrets

One parent says,

- "This weekend we really had a good time. But I think it would be a good idea not to tell [other parent]. I don't want to hurt their feelings."

- "I haven't told [other parent] yet, but I'm going to take you on a cruise this summer. Don't say anything. Let me talk to [him/her] first. I think it would be better that way."

- "As far as I'm concerned, it's okay if you have a beer when you're with me. You're sixteen, and I know other kids drink. I'd rather you be home with me instead of out with your friends drinking. Just don't tell [other parent]. They wouldn't understand."

- "[Other parent] doesn't know it yet, but I just got a wide-screen TV. You know we probably shouldn't say anything, because they might just get jealous."

- "Yes, you're right. My new friend did sleep over last night in my bedroom. I'll talk about it to [other parent] when the time is right. It's not something you should have to talk to them about."

If one of your parents asked you to keep a secret from the other, you probably had a hard time resolving this dilemma. If you kept the secret, you were being loyal to that parent. But, what if the other parent asked you about the secret? Who should you be loyal to then? You could only maintain the loyalty of one parent at a time. If you maintained the confidence of one parent, you were not being loyal to the other parent. You were either forced to lie to that parent or say there was a secret that you couldn't disclose. Both of these last two choices are also difficult. The lie leaves you feeling guilty, and saying you cannot disclose the secret puts you in the position of stirring up the conflict between your parents. The second parent may then go on to try to discover the secret. Either way, you are in a no-win situation and in the midst of a highly emotional and complex problem that you, as a child, shouldn't have to face.

Revealing Parental Mistakes

While your parent may have asked you to keep a secret at times, there may have been other instances when *you* may have decided to have a secret or even to lie to one parent to protect the other from the wrath or onslaught of the other. What would you have done and how would you have felt in the following situations?

- One of your parents was given a traffic ticket for driving under the influence of alcohol.

- The parent you were with forgot to pick you up after an extracurricular event.

- One parent forgot to give you your medicine.

- One parent did not take you to Sunday school.

Parents inevitably make mistakes. They can use poor judgement, be unreliable, get too angry, try unsuccessfully to be deceptive, and so on. They may even do something appropriate but that goes against the desires or values of the child or the other parent and is seen as a mistake.

Were the mistakes of one of your parents secrets to be kept from the other? Were you asked not to tell? Were you questioned (or interrogated) by one parent about what happened while you were with the other? If you volunteered information about something, was that used by one parent against the other? Was disclosing information a way to forge an alliance with or get extra support from one parent?

Here again, children are put in a no-win situation. It is difficult for a child to get support from one parent if talking about the mistake of the other parent is going to feel like a betrayal or lead to more conflict between the parents. If your parents were not committed to collaborating in child rearing, they might also have put pressure on you not to tell about a mistake. They might also have been less likely to admit the error, as admitting a mistake could lead them to be in a compromised legal position. Unfortunately, children in these situations are not free to just be children because they are forced to make adult decisions.

Loving Parents Who Don't Love Each Other

Imagine someone criticizes your best friend, significant other, or your own child. Imagine if they actually dislike the person you love. Whose side are you on? Generally, the answer to this question is easy. However, for children of divorce this answer is not at all easy when one parent seems to hate the other. The adult in the above example usually has little to no allegiance to the attacking person. All of the allegiance is to the loved one. Unfortunately, the child of divorce doesn't have the same clarity. If you were in this position, you know the difficulty of having to listen to the criticisms of one or both of your parents against the other. You again could easily feel as if you were betraying one parent and consequently being torn apart. The problem is made worse when you realize that the essence of who you are is made up from both of your parents (from both biological and personality perspectives). If each parent says that the other is hated and unworthy of love, and you are part of both parents, then what part of you is left that is worthy of being loved?

These choices and conflicts are so damaging for children. Children love both parents in spite of each parent's problems, weaknesses, and mistakes. Parents are the center of children's lives, giving the children their framework for viewing the world and themselves. Right or wrong, children rely on their parents for a sense of stability, love, and value.

Your parents' divorce may have been stressful and traumatic in and of itself, simply as a result of your family's reconfiguration into two households. However, if you faced the choices we've described above, you had even more stress. Unwittingly, parents and the system have put children into these impossible binds. Parents fight with each other over the best interests of the child but then look to the child to put the bullets in the gun as they go to war against one another.

The Effects of Loyalty Conflicts

Loyalty conflicts aren't just unfair. They don't just put children in difficult situations. No, they can be far more damaging. They can cause significant stress and negative emotions, making you feel insecure and unsafe in your relationships with your parents. Loyalty conflicts can, as we describe in this section, also impact your feelings about yourself and your own adult relationships.

Double Binds

Loyalty conflicts put children (of any age) in double binds. A double bind is a situation in which the person gets conflicting information or has conflicting choices such that there is no apparent right answer or way to win. It's a "damned if you do, damned if you don't" situation. Double binds can cause intense emotional stress and a strong desire to escape the situation.

★ *To Hurt or to Lie*

Peter returns to Mom's house after spending the weekend with Dad. Mom asks, "How was your weekend? What did you do with your father?" Peter wants to tell Mom that he had a wonderful time at the amusement park with Dad, but if he does, Mom will be upset and jealous. She may even make a derogatory comment about Dad, such as "Since he's left, he thinks he can buy your love with money. What does he know about really being a parent?" If Peter keeps the joy he had over the weekend to himself, he has to lie to Mom by saying "Okay, not much." Or, he can say, "Well, we went to an amusement park, but it wasn't very good. I really missed you." In this example, Peter is feeling the pressure to take care of his mother's feelings. Sometimes this pressure can be so strong that the child will resist going to the other parent's home just to spare the first parent pain.

★

So, the child of divorce is in a difficult bind. They can share the joy and thereby hurt the other parent. Or the child can lie, keeping their feelings inside and in some way making the parent with whom they spent the weekend look bad. Either way, the child is put in the position of having to choose which parent they are going to hurt. Children know that they deserve to be out of the middle of a loyalty conflict. They can sense that there is something wrong when they can't freely enjoy themselves with one parent and be honest with the other.

This type of situation can occur over and over again for children. As you think about your own childhood, think about the number of times you were in similar situations. How did it make you feel? How did you cope?

Even as adults, children of divorce can find themselves in these binds. This may be most evident at major life events. For example, was high school or college graduation difficult? With whom did you celebrate? Did you feel like you were in the middle or did your parents spare you that awkwardness and celebrate together with you or make up the schedule themselves?

Many adult children of divorce will talk about their own weddings and how difficult it was to figure out how to deal with both their parents being present. They struggle with questions such as, "Who is going to walk me down the aisle?" or "Where am I going to seat them?" or "How am I going to deal with my stepparents being present? When Dad sees my stepfather he's going to throw a fit." Even years after the divorce, parents still put their children in the middle, burdening an otherwise happy and special time with issues of their own divorce. Somehow, someway, the child's wedding turns into being about the parents' divorce, where many decisions are still viewed as representing the child's love for or loyalty to one or the other parent.

Even the birth of a grandchild can be an occasion for more discomfort as the new parents have to think about and plan when the grandparents can visit. They have to feel the anxiety about both parents and perhaps their current spouses all being present at the same time. Who will talk to whom? What will be said? Are you going to call Dad's wife "grandma" or is that term reserved just for Mom? Here again, the issues of the divorce upstage the joy of the new grandchild as they insert themselves into the dynamics, thoughts, and feelings of today.

Throughout the years, the consequences of these repeated conflicts take their toll on the child of divorce. Intense feelings can begin subtly and later become more pronounced. They can be directed at yourself or your parents or even impact your new relationships. Notice, if you will, how these feelings parallel those of the divorcing parents discussed in chapter 2.

Anxiety

One of the primary emotional responses to a double bind is anxiety. This is contributed to by the child's belief that parents are supposed to take care of them and keep them safe. When a child is caught in loyalty conflicts, they feel far from safe. Not only can the child be made to feel responsible for hurting one parent or the other, but the child can feel like it's not safe to just be themselves. Expressing emotions, stating the facts of a situation, telling one parent about something important that happened while you were with the other parent are all opportunities for the danger signals to go off. Someone is going to get hurt. The normal feeling that occurs when we suspect physical or emotional danger is anxiety. Anxiety over the long term can lead us to feel nervous, have problems sleeping and concentrating, and can cause physical problems. Anxiety can lead us to want to escape from the situation (run away from home) or get angry and fight (throw a tantrum).

Over the long term, ongoing anxiety can lead a person to feel like they are frequently on guard, worrying, or brooding. Little things can trigger excessive anxiety if you have spent years experiencing the world as threatening or scary.

Anger

An adult child of divorce wants to tell her father about her mother's recent illness. She begins to talk to Dad when his wife walks into the room. Dad gets very uncomfortable. His wife apologizes for walking into a "private" discussion and exits the room. Dad says, "I hope your mother feels better soon." He then ends the conversation quickly and goes into the other room to talk to his wife. The child is left feeling horribly unsupported and as if she has put her father in an awkward position with his new wife.

One ten-year-old succinctly expressed her viewpoint as a loyalty-conflict victim of her parents' divorce: "It's hard enough not having my parents together. Why do they have to stand on different sides of the soccer field? When I make a goal, I have to decide who to look at first. Should I look to this side or that side? Who do I go to at the end of the game? Do I go to Mom who came to my game when it's not her weekend, since I know she's really missing me? Or do I go with Dad, who I'm supposed to be with? Why do *I* have to choose?"

The anger can build and build, especially after hundreds of these types of situations. Some children feel free to express this anger, while others feel they don't have the right or freedom to do so. These children (of any age) bottle up the anger, believing they may hurt or even lose their parents (or other loved ones) if they express it. This anger can spill out in other relationships of adult children of divorce. You may find that you get frustrated easily and have little tolerance for the usual disappointments of life.

Depression

Depression is a normal response to loss, and loyalty conflicts can intensify the feelings of loss that the divorce has caused. Not only has the family been reconfigured, but the child involved is not in the position to be the "child." They have to worry about the subtleties of communicating with their parents on the soccer field. They may also worry about whether or not to be honest, and whether or not to ask one parent about something related to the other parent. In a sense, the child has become more of the adult and has indeed had another loss. That is, the child has lost a piece of their own childhood.

Depression can be mild and of short duration. However, it can also be more acutely intense and last a long time. It can affect your feelings about yourself, your eating and sleeping patterns, energy, and even your will to live. Professional help is often indicated when the feelings of depression are intense, long lasting, or affecting your day-to-day functioning.

Guilt

If you've experienced loyalty conflicts and the sense that in some way you hurt one or both of your parents by your actions, how can you avoid feeling guilty? Do you think somehow the ten-year-old on the soccer field got the message from her parents that it mattered who she looked at first, or who she went to at the end of the game? Sure she did. Likewise, she got the message that it really mattered who she did *not* look at first or go to at the end of the game. She learned that her actions made a difference to the happiness of her parents.

You can hear her mother saying, "You know, you're going to be with your father the rest of the weekend. I really miss you and just want to give you a hug right away. I have to wait the whole weekend for you to come back. I just don't want to wait right now, too."

And you can hear her father saying almost the same thing to her, "You know, this is *my* weekend with you. I waited all week to be with you. This is our time. I don't mind your mother being here for your game, but I shouldn't have to wait for you to hug her when it's our time to be together."

Whatever the child does, one of the people she loves feels bad. How can she not feel guilty when she is told that she has caused one or both of her parents pain?

While guilt in this situation is expected, it is unnecessary. The child didn't do anything wrong. She was just caught up in her parents' conflict and tug-of-war. As an adult, it's important to avoid taking on the guilt associated with others' comments and actions. You need to ask, "What have I *really* done that was wrong?"

Low Self-Esteem

The cumulative impact of all these feelings brought about by loyalty conflicts can be low self-esteem. Instead of feeling loved and nurtured, in spite of your parents' divorce, do you feel responsible and bad about yourself? If so, you too may have been caught in too many loyalty conflicts. Some parents can teach their children that they are worthwhile. Yet, if you feel like you have repeatedly betrayed one or both parents, how can you feel good about yourself? Your parents can tell you they're proud of you and that you're special, but you know different. The effect of the loyalty conflict is to make you feel guilty and disrespect yourself because you know inside yourself about the secrets you've held and the trust you feel you have breached.

It is even harder to feel good about yourself if you were put in the position where you believe it is your fault that your parents feel bad. Are you saying as you read this, "How can I like myself when I made Mom or Dad feel even worse than they already do about being divorced. What kind of child would do this to their parents?" If this has a familiar ring to it, it is likely you may have been caught in some loyalty conflicts.

Distrust of Parental Relationships

Parents are supposed to take care of their children, not the other way around. Unfortunately, our ten-year-old friend on the soccer field can't even enjoy her game without worrying about taking care of Mom and Dad in the process. Furthermore, she can't trust that it is okay to just be the child. Mom and Dad are not protecting her childhood and are not protecting her from their own feelings about the divorce and their own adult issues and needs. It's very hard to trust your parents when you do not feel protected by them.

Trust can also erode from a lack of consistency in the behavior of your parents toward you. For example, sometimes they could have felt loving and supportive. Yet, without warning, you could have become immersed into the game of divorce espionage, when it feels like your parent is torturing you to tell all.

Impact on Adult Loving Relationships

Steven, a twenty-seven-year-old whose parents had a high-conflict divorce says, "My parents getting divorced hasn't affected me. Actually, it's helped me better understand relationships. When I meet a woman, I know she's not what she seems. Everyone is after something. Either she's going to take advantage of me and get what she wants or I'm going to get what I want. That's the difference between me and my friends whose parents haven't divorced. I've learned what it's all about. I was caught in the middle, so I don't trust anyone. I learned choosing means losing."

What has happened to Steven? Sure, he has grown up fast. He has learned some powerful lessons from being caught in loyalty binds. He has learned not to trust relationships and to take what he can get. We can just imagine how he would have difficulty being genuine in a relationship. He would also not easily trust the other person. It is easy to see how he might go from relationship to relationship only finding (from his perspective) more evidence to "prove" that these concepts about relationships are right. Each failed relationship can be "evidence" of how being vulnerable, nurturing, or trusting cannot possibly be of value. Each failed relationship only proves to him that relationships cannot be long-term or lasting. We would expect him to think, "It's just a matter of time before it's going to fall apart. They all do."

In short, the loyalty conflicts you were potentially caught in as a child may have had very significant effects on how you view yourself, your parents, and your adult relationships. You may still be caught in these same conflicts if you're in contact with one or both of your parents. In the second half of this book, we will discuss how to deal with some of the feelings that the loyalty conflicts may have caused and how to try to limit their impact on you and on your adult relationships.

Chapter 5

New Parental Relationships

Just when you thought your parents' divorce was more than enough to handle, along comes your parent's new "friend." The adjustment to your parents being single is one thing, but to trying to integrate a new relationship or multiple new relationships is quite another. One of the most difficult parts of dealing with your parent's new romantic partners is that it again signals the end of the marriage. Whether young or old, children of divorce often maintain reunification fantasies. Although you may not consciously acknowledge that you wanted your parents' lives to stay the same, you may have been shocked to see your parents begin to move forward in some ways, and that means dating, too. This stage and its possible movement toward a permanent new relationship can be disconcerting and confusing for children of divorce.

Two Family Units

After a divorce, two new family units are formed with you, your siblings, and each parent. It's important for these new units to have time to establish their own identity and settle into their own routines. Even without new partners, single parents struggle with many of their own issues while their children have to get used to the absence of the other parent. These adjustments are logistical, emotional, and financial, as each household takes time to form or reconfigure life with one parent instead of two. When these changes are well integrated, the family circle closes around both households and once again goes on its way. The introduction of new dating partners or significant others penetrates the new family unit and requires the parent and children to adjust again to another major change and the inclusion of these strangers.

As you think about the new adults that came into one or both of your parents' lives, it may be helpful to complete the brief journal exercise below.

Journal Exercise 5.1

In the space below, rate on a 1 to 5 scale the following items.

	Disagree				Agree
The introduction of my parent's "friend" was a surprise to me.	1	2	3	4	5
I didn't like my parent's significant other(s).	1	2	3	4	5
I was jealous of the time my parent spent with this person.	1	2	3	4	5
I felt like I had to keep this relationship from my other parent.	1	2	3	4	5
When my parent's new relationship ended, I was hurt by the loss.	1	2	3	4	5
Our home was turned upside-down when this person moved in.	1	2	3	4	5
This new relationship worsened our financial situation.	1	2	3	4	5
My relationships with my stepsiblings were difficult.	1	2	3	4	5

Now, total your scores for all items. The higher your total score, the more likely it is that you may have been negatively affected by your parent's new relationship. Although the issues for children may vary somewhat according to their age level, some of the effects are quite stable and enduring.

Mother or Father versus Man or Woman

Adult children of divorce struggle with changing their perception of their parents as "Mom" or "Dad" to individuals with their own adult needs for relationships and intimacy. This is a very difficult shift as you must try to preserve your parent/child relationship, while at the same time accepting your parent's adult needs. Certainly as a child and even now as an adult, you may choose and need to view your parents in their roles as your caretakers and protectors and not as men and women with their own needs, desires, and wants. The very idea that they may be independent and sexual beings can be alien and may even feel threatening to your sense of security. Not only did the divorce change your world, but look at your parents now! You still may be upset about the divorce, while they are happily "in love."

In addition to viewing your parents as adults with needs of their own, the child of divorce also may re-experience a kind of separation anxiety analogous to that of the eight-month-old child who is learning how to negotiate the world away from the immediate protection of parents. You may wonder about your parent's "other" life. This certainly occurs when you're not with that parent on weekends, weekdays, vacations, and so on, but it also occurs when you are with that parent and they are engaging with others as the new man or woman you never knew. You may wonder, "Just what are they doing when I'm not around?" You can feel like you are losing touch with what is left of the very foundation of your security. You can experience anxiety, hurt, fear, a lack of control, and a sense of abandonment all in the course of one night or one weekend, let alone over years since the divorce. The appropriate balance between a parent's new life and relationships and their children is the essence of the solution. The prolonged re-experience of separation anxiety may last well into adulthood, leaving you with a profound sense of loss and an inability to commit to anyone who might leave you again. Not only can the divorce itself engender these types of commitment phobias, but the second premature loss of your parent to a new significant other or even to the roller-coaster world of dating post divorce can leave you with the same worries and avoidance behavior.

A New Friend?

Everybody needs friends, right? That means even your parents. You can understand this because your own friends are vitally important to you. You may have said to yourself, "I thought Mom and Dad already had friends, so why the new ones? Why do these new friends have to be here during my time with Mom/Dad, and why do they have to have new children for us to have to play with and make our new friends, too?" You might have thought that, although your parents may think that they need these new friends, *you* surely do not. Besides, they do not always act like friends, so what is a "new friend" anyway?

★   *"Friend"?*

In Tamara's divorcing family, Dad had a new friend who had been introduced to the children fairly early on in the divorce process. Since Mom believed that this relationship had been the catalyst for the divorce, she did not appreciate the involvement of the children with this woman and had great difficulty accepting her role. Tamara's dad brought her everywhere, eventually became engaged and remarried, and had two new children with his "friend." Throughout this entire time, from dating to engagement to remarriage and after, Tamara never used the first name of Dad's friend but instead was encouraged to call her just "friend." Yes, that continues to be her name as stepmother! Tamara and her siblings call her "friend." This woman never was just a friend and the confusion will continue to disturb Tamara her whole life.

★

"This Is My New Friend"

When a divorced parent says these words, a new world has begun. Dozens of questions start to run through the mind of a child, adolescent, and even an adult. To list a few:

- Who is this person?

- When did my parent meet them and where?

- How long has this been going on?

- Does this new friend have any children?

- How does my parent feel about them?

- What will my other parent think, feel, and say?

- Will my parent love them more than me?

- Will my parent divorce *me* because they love this other person?

Parents are often not prepared to answer these questions and at the same time help their children with their feelings. There are ways to minimize the possible negative effects of introducing new relationships to children of divorce and maximize the positive aspects. Some of these issues have been addressed in chapter 10 of *The Co-Parenting Survival Guide* (Thayer and Zimmerman 2001). See how many of these strategies one or both of your parents used.

Waiting

Children of divorce, no matter how old, are not necessarily in need of their parents' new friends. These individuals are usually providing companionship to the parent, yet children do not need to know about them too soon. If parents introduce new friends to children too early, they run the risk of exposing the children to new and maybe multiple losses. Were you left out of the equation until your parents were more stabilized in the new relationship? Did you slowly get to know their significant other at the right time? Or were you thrown into the new relationship? How did that feel?

Balancing

The introduction of new relationships upsets the new balance between parent and child postdivorce. Two new family units are formed with one parent at the helm of each. The new family wheel should learn to turn together first before new friends expand that wheel. New relationships take time, energy, focus, finances, and other resources to maintain, and thus they take some of these same resources away from the new postdivorce family unit. In other words, if new relationships were introduced too early or without regard for balancing the effects upon the new family unit, you could have experienced a profound sense of loneliness and disregard, causing you to feel angry and depressed. Did your parents balance time alone with you and your siblings with the involvement of their new friends?

One glaring example of this kind of disregard for the concept of balance occurred in one family wherein both mother and father introduced new significant others to the children within a few months of the divorce. Dad, in fact, had not spent an entire weekend with the children alone since the divorce was final. When it came time for Dad to take the children for his first vacation postdivorce, his friend came along for the entire time. How do you think the children felt? Was this in their best interests? Would you have felt you were important to this dad? In a parent counseling session, Dad was asked to reflect upon whether bringing his new girlfriend along was done for him or for his children. He was assured by the counselor that this was his need and certainly not his children's.

Avoiding Loyalty Issues

The involvement of a parent's new relationship in the lives of children postdivorce is not a private matter. It will get back to the other parent, to be sure. This puts children in a difficult position because they are often the first to disclose the secret. It creates loyalty conflicts for children of any age and asks them to bear the feelings of the other parent upon that discovery. If you felt like you had to choose between your loyalty to each parent, did you choose the parent who was alone because they didn't have anyone else? Or did you choose the parent who had a new relationship for fear that this new person and maybe their family would try to take the parent away? Could you disclose that you liked one parent's new partner to the other parent? When faced with new relationships too soon, children of divorce are left in untenable positions that can create major difficulty in trusting their judgments about making secure and unfettered choices in relationships.

Knowing Whose House Is Whose

The physical space of the postdivorce family residences probably required some adjustment, redecorating, and just plain getting used to. When new romantic attachments start to spend lots of time with parents, they also change the dynamics of the physical space. They may even start to bring their things over and leave them there or introduce new items that look "just right" and rearrange things. If this happened in your family, you may have noticed that your home just didn't feel like "home" anymore. If your parent disregarded your timetable by hopping into a new relationship too soon, you may continue to feel confused about ownership of your own physical space. You might notice that you are possessive and rigid about your own physical space and belongings, and that you have difficulty sharing with even those whom you love. Conversely, you can be too passive with others, feeling like you don't have the right to say no and assert your right to establish personal boundaries, even within your own home.

Avoiding Major Financial Problems

Finances are often a big issue in any divorce, causing excessive conflict and legal involvement. Children of divorce, no matter what age, are frequently overexposed to the details and emotional turmoil of their parents' financial settlements. Money can be used as a wedge, a weapon used against the other parent, or as the ultimate prize for loyalty and affection. Money issues sometime leave children of divorce feeling uncertain about their security with one or both parents and concerned about the stability of their own future. When new relationships are introduced, the result can either enhance the financial situation (but sometimes with strings attached) or it can reduce the money in the pot, which now has to be shared with others.

If finances were tight, you may have felt that your parent's expenditures on their new relationship were unwarranted and took away from your needs being addressed. Unfortunately, you may also have heard these sentiments echoed by your other parent and even from extended family and friends. "Dad seems to have enough money to take Sue to the Caribbean islands, but he can't even take you guys to the Cape for a weekend in the summer!" Or, "Mom is always crying poor to me, saying that she doesn't have enough money to buy you new sneakers for school. But she seems to be able to go to New York with her new boyfriend any time she pleases!" Or, "Mom never bought tickets to the theater before. I wonder who paid for all of that, her new boyfriend?"

With input like this, no wonder children of divorce don't know whom to support. Even if they like the new romantic partner, they don't know whether to be open to that person, for fear of upsetting the other parent and maybe their own future. They also don't know whether to feel free to accept gifts and other offerings from a parent's generous new friend for fear that they will be dependent upon them and perhaps incur the wrath, rejection, and hurt of the other parent.

Preparing for New Siblings

You may have thought that you had your own room finally, all to yourself. Your desk was just the way you wanted it and your stereo was perfect, with your CD collection in place. The posters were up in your new house and your "Keep Out" sign was on the door. Even your little sister couldn't get in without knocking. Then there was a strange knock at the door and strange voices, too. Your Dad said, "Bobby, let us in please. I have someone special here for you to meet." You opened the door and there was Dad's new girlfriend with her six-year-old son.

It may be one thing to have to get used to your parent's new friend, but it's quite another to accept their children into your home. This could have resulted in a positive experience or it could have felt like an intrusion into your new family unit and a disruption of the equilibrium established in your parent's home after the divorce. This is even more of an issue if your parent's new partner has children, and they come too. Rooms might have had to be shared, couches could have become beds, and even your toothbrush might not have been safe in its usual spot in the bathroom. Did your parents introduce the children of new friends carefully and slowly so that the parent/child relationship was respected and preserved? Did all the children have a chance to get acquainted and to make their own unrushed judgments? If not, you may have been faced with even more feelings of displacement and loss, not to mention questions about your parent's priorities.

We're Getting Married!

Okay, so maybe you felt like you could get used to the "new friend" idea and maybe even those kids that came with it, but *married*? You've got to be kidding! That was asking way too much. The decision by a parent to remarry can be traumatic but it could have also been an opportunity to learn about relationships in a healthy manner. The direction that this decision takes depends very much upon the way in which your parent and the potential new stepparent introduced and nurtured the relationship within the boundaries and needs of the divorced family unit. Children of divorce whose reactions are not respected or recognized are more likely to continue to react negatively to the new marriage well beyond the wedding and maybe even into adulthood. Others, who have been included in the process in an age-appropriate manner and whose parent and future stepparent have demonstrated a good balance between the divorced family units and the new blended family unit, may have had their lives expanded and enhanced in many positive ways.

Tell Them Congratulations for Me

The remarriage of a parent usually sends the final signal that the old marriage has ended. Because of reunification fantasies, it is very hard to let go of the old dreams. Even the stark reality of separate homes, separate vacations, new relationships, and time apart do not completely eradicate these strong desires. The announcement of a remarriage by either parent throws cold water on those dreams and desires for a reunified family. Children of divorce are also sometimes thrown back into the old tense and hostile exchanges that occurred early on in the divorce. Higher-conflict parents may revert back to their old bitter and argumentative ways and drag the children in too, especially if the kids are now adults themselves. In fact, adult children of divorce may find that they feel like children again, caught up in the tennis match of their parents' conflict.

Did your parents experience a resurgence of old and mixed feelings such as

- *Anger:* life is going on for my ex and not for me

- *Worry:* about the stepfamily, finances, the quality of the coparenting relationship

- *Jealousy:* old feelings of rejection and maybe even envy

- *Hurt:* especially if the new marriage came as a surprise

Not all these mixed feelings are painful though. For example, some may be positive.

- *Relief:* that there is a good new stepparent to help with the child care

- *Happiness:* a genuine sense of well wishes and congratulations

- *Hope:* for a better coparenting relationship and maybe even hope for their own relationship future

If your other parent could have some or all of these feelings, then surely you can too.

Did your parents talk parent to parent first and not have the children be the conduits for this important information? Adult children of divorce may actually feel more trapped in this bind than younger children. Parents need to take responsibility for their own decisions and to be willing to cope directly with the emotional consequences.

On the other hand, if your parents did this well, took the time to pay attention to others and not just themselves, took plenty of time building the relationship, allowed themselves to understand the reactions of the other parent, and tried hard to find the right balance between their old family unit, their coparenting relationship, and their future spouse and family, then remarriage could have been a step toward furthering the postdivorce healing process. It can also have expanded your world to include others who love and care about you. Your world could have become a larger and broader place than before. Perhaps you learned that adults can make difficult choices and go on to change their lives in successful ways.

Let the Blending Begin

Families can increase just a little or they can increase exponentially when remarriage occurs. Parents and stepparents can accomplish this blending while being attentive to the feelings and effects upon all involved directly and peripherally, or they can just assume it will all work out and go forth without a whole lot of consideration. Blending families takes time and respect for all to have successful results. Once again, the preservation of the original parent/child postdivorce family relationship is essential, along with the integration of the new stepfamily members. Too much of one or the other in blended families can throw the scales off balance and result in a mixture of confusing and unsorted feelings for children of divorce.

Physical Space

The house naturally gets smaller when more people move in. Did your parents plan carefully when they created the new arrangements? Creativity is imperative and providing places to get away but also places to integrate is essential. The loss of your personal space and privacy can easily carry over as major issues into your adulthood. You may not make the best roommate in a communal living situation because you can either feel that you have to protect your "corner" at all costs, creating boundaries, locked doors, and "Keep Out" signs, or you can feel that you have little to no say in protecting your space, your belongings, or your haven from the intrusion of others. You might be considered easy to live with, or you can be an easy target for being taken advantage by others. Your roommates or spouse may not appreciate all those loafers who camp out on your couch to the point where their toothbrushes have a permanent spot in the bathroom holder.

Finances

When there is enough money to go around, then the financial issues in blended families are of lesser import. Sometimes the finances even improve when stepfamilies integrate because expenses consolidate and income may increase from the additional salary or child support of a new spouse. Yet, even this can create some problems for children of divorce. If the new stepparent is now the major breadwinner, authority and control issues may change dramatically. The financial support and generosity of one adult can now contaminate your feelings about your stepparents. This can create such confusion that you may not be able to sort out how you really feel about the parent. Instead, you may find the relationship is built upon the give-and-take of material objects and not on more authentic and deeper emotions.

More often, though, this is not the case, as the integration of stepfamilies brings about a change in the finances that requires more frugality and financial vigilance. There are usually more people and less money to go around. Women usually lose their alimony upon remarriage, while the spouse paying child support continues to have the same financial obligations to their ex-spouse. Children of divorce can easily feel destabilized when finances are called into question and are again a matter of contention between parents. Adult children of divorce are not immune to this either. You may see one of your parents struggling to make ends meet, while your other parent enjoys a much more luxurious lifestyle. You may also feel guilty that your own life is more stable than that of one parent and see a role reversal take place earlier than would be developmentally expected, with you now financially taking care of your parent.

Of course, an even more serious effect occurs when there is no longer enough money to go around. If finances determined whether or not you went to college, went on a family vacation, went to camp or to the movies, had new school clothes, or even had your favorite foods to eat, you could have felt resentful and angry. This may have made the integration of your new stepfamily even more difficult.

These struggles can leave you feeling confused and insecure about financial issues as an adult. The changes in the financial structure of your family may lead to a strong need to make sure that your own income does not falter. You may decide that you never want to feel that insecure again and thus make work and money the major priorities in your life, eclipsing family and other relationships and even other avocations and fun. You also may choose to be involved in a relationship where your financial future is more certain at the expense of choosing a partner in life with whom you can grow emotionally and intimately. That might, in essence, kill two birds with one stone by ensuring that you replicate the lack of intimacy you saw between your parents in your own relationship, while at the same time establishing a level of financial dependence upon your partner that creates an imbalance in the relationship. Maybe you are looking for the parent/child security that was disrupted, but you will certainly not find it this way. You could instead decide that this whole money thing is just not worth it and opt for a simpler life freer of financial obligations, perhaps forgoing others who would depend upon you for their support—like a spouse and children. This would again let you avoid having to establish the intimacy that real interdependent relationships require and even enjoy.

Just Who Is in Charge?

A remarriage can confuse the structure of decision making and authority if your parents let it happen. Even if stepparents are primary caretakers or just wonderful people who love you and want what is best for you in an unbiased manner, they are still not the ones who should have made the major decisions about your life. They should ideally have been your parents' very valuable and directly involved consultants, but not in charge. Hopefully, they had a cooperative level of communication with your other parent, but the discussions about who you were, whether you needed braces or a tutor, or if you should play soccer, basketball, or both should really have been left up to your parents. Stepparents can have a lot of input, but the last word should not have been theirs. This way of working together requires parents to think ahead about how to balance the needs of new stepfamilies with the needs of their own children and the other parent. Even making a decision to participate in an extracurricular activity can affect the schedule and plans of both parents and thus the schedule and plans of possibly both new stepfamilies. The parents are the information gatherers through whom decisions should have been processed and implemented.

This also pertains to discipline. Parents should decide major disciplinary matters together, hopefully in some sort of unified manner. Then it is the job of both families to implement each decision. This is especially true for adolescents who know how to push the envelope and how to manipulate two parents even when their parents remain married and are living together. Communication and consistency are keys to good discipline. The ultimate authority should have been in the hands of your parents, divorced or not.

When these roles get confused, it can really confuse children of divorce. Remember that your parents probably told you that, in spite of their divorce, they would always be parents together for you and your siblings. Well, a lack of clear distinction in authority can leave you feeling like this promise was violated and that your new stepparent can easily sway your parent's alliances. Whom did you petition when you wanted to stay out later, change your schedule, or pick your summer job? As a child of divorce, did you lose that direct connection to your parent? Did you lose respect for your parent, who you saw as "brainwashed" by their spouse, and then ally with your other parent? If so, this may have severely altered your relationship with your parents. Stepparents should remain stepparents and your parents should remain parents so children of divorce can have them both in their lives without resentment. All parent figures have important roles to play in your development, but your life play could not have run smoothly if they all stepped on each other's toes and said each other's lines.

A New Stepfamily Multiplied by How Much?

Well, if you thought it was confusing and complicated introducing one new stepparent and their children, then what about two, three, or more? When parents engage in serial marriages and divorces, their children are exposed to multiple adjustments and losses, sometimes building up calluses on their emotions in the process.

It's extremely hard for children of divorce to allow themselves to become attached and connected to new stepparents and stepsiblings and then to see them leave as a parent divorces again. This is just one important reason to use slow introductions and take plenty of time to get to know each other. The unfortunate lesson for children of divorce may then be that relationships are unstable creatures, so why bother, or if you do, why invest all the way? This can lead to the "committed relationship phobia" that has been associated with adult children of divorce (Wallerstein, Lewis, and Blakeslee 2001). It's easy to understand how you would feel reluctant to give your heart away again and again. The choice of being alone or only engaging in more superficial relationships may seem much more appealing. Children of divorce who are exposed to multiple divorces may never really learn firsthand how a healthy relationship is structured and how to keep it going in spite of the ups and downs of life. They may have a pessimistic view of the possibility of ever being able to sustain an intimate relationship and may even sabotage the good ones when the time comes to truly say yes.

★ *Jessica's Phobia*

Jessica has been dating Frank for about three and a half years. They are in their early twenties. It is a good relationship that has grown over the years. Jessica is amazed that, unlike her parents, who suddenly divorced about ten years ago and then divorced again within five years, she and Frank really seem to have "it." They can be together for days without fighting. They take long walks together. They seem to read each other's mind and finish each other's sentences. Frank is caring and considerate and really seems to love her. Their friends see them as "the perfect couple," and their parents have joked about when Frank will finally pop the question.

Last night Frank and Jessica went to a wonderful, small, quiet restaurant and Frank quietly and romantically began to talk about getting married. Jessica immediately became anxious and frightened. She had trouble breathing and felt panicky. She told Frank she couldn't ever imagine being with someone else but also couldn't imagine having the level of commitment that marriage would require. She didn't want to end up like her parents and raise children in a family of divorce. She knew Frank couldn't guarantee that they wouldn't get divorced and just felt like it wasn't fair to put children in that position. She told Frank that he might want to think about seeing someone else if he thought he might want to get married, because she didn't know whether she could ever marry him or anyone.

★

As in the above example with Frank, it is a lot of work for a partner in a relationship with an adult child of divorce. They need to have secure egos, good self-esteem, lots of patience, and healthy relationships in their own backgrounds. You may try very hard to sink them, reject them, put them down, and test them endlessly as you seek to have them prove they really will stay. Alternatively, you may try to prove you are right and that it is just a matter of time before they will inevitably leave.

Your Fault—Again?

Multiple losses through parents' multiple divorces can also continue to replicate the childhood assumption that you contributed to the demise of your parents' marriages. This can leave you questioning your own worth and evaluating yourself in an overly self-critical manner. You believe that the main consistent factor in all your parents' interactions is you. It seems to you that if you weren't so stupid, angry, ugly, rude, difficult, or such a nuisance, your parents' relationships would have lasted. Of course then, if you feel that you really don't deserve that wonderful partner or that you will somehow destroy the relationship and hurt them anyway, then you may not embark upon this territory for anything. We will again address the effects of parent divorce on adult intimate relationships in more detail in chapter 9.

Staying Close

One of the other issues resulting from multiple divorces is how to maintain relationships with multiple families. The prospect of losing a caring stepparent and maybe some stepsiblings can feel devastating. Even though stepparents and children have good intentions to remain connected and see each other regularly, it just isn't the same. The logistics of balancing a parenting plan with two biological parents is hard enough, but adding in one or more stepfamilies becomes exponentially more complicated and next to impossible. If we throw in an adolescent's own need for independence and peer relationships or an adult child's busy work life and maybe their own family, the logistics can be insurmountable. What were once valuable, caring relationships may now be relegated to casual, infrequent contacts and holiday cards. If parent-to-stepparent conflict was high during the second divorce, then children of divorce may not have much of a say about whether they remain in touch with stepfamilies.

This is especially true for younger children. As an adult, you can more easily exercise your own desires, but this may be at the expense of your relationship with one or both of your biological parents.

First you are encouraged, maybe even required, to foster a relationship with your new stepfamily members, and then you are told that you should not see them, talk to them, or continue to contact them in any way. How confusing is that? It can also set up a power struggle between you and your parent as you desperately try to hold onto the good parts of your new life. Maybe that stepparent was always there for you in a way that your parents were not. Or maybe an older stepsibling taught you to ski and always helped you with your math homework. Perhaps your stepparent buffered the conflict between your parents. You may feel very resentful that you have to lose all this just because your parent cannot sustain a committed relationship. The transitory nature of life is again all too familiar. It can seem to characterize your childhood life and can then also characterize your adult life if you choose to repeat these same patterns. The likelihood of this repetitive process is high, especially if you don't have some understanding of the effects of your parents' divorce or divorces upon your adult choices for partners. Ignorance and naivete can result in the reemergence of the same old pattern in your own life and that of your own children.

Unfortunately, the concept of family has not progressed enough yet to encompass a wide range of diversity. The amount of litigation relative to the number of predivorce parent education and counseling programs speaks volumes about the status of promoting cooperative divorce coparenting. Therefore, our culture's acceptance of multiple divorces and routinely offering children help acclimating to those changes still seems light years away. We don't need to promote serial marriages, but we do need to understand the effect upon children both during the divorce itself, throughout childhood, and into adulthood. That is the only way that we can begin to positively impact the process and perhaps interfere with its feared legacy.

The Good, the Bad, and the Ugly

You thought that dealing with your parents' divorce was complicated and now it seems even more intricate with the introduction of all these new people into your life. Let's first underscore the idea that stepparents, stepsiblings, and extended stepfamily members can be wonderful and enriching additions to your life. When remarriage works well, parents and children have a real second chance to learn about relationships in a healthy way. Children in these families have firsthand knowledge of not only what can go wrong in committed relationships, but also how to do it right. Their world is enhanced and expanded with the introduction of new personalities, new ideas, and more people who love and care for them. Children can learn much about conflict resolution, cooperation, parenting, flexibility, independence, and love from parents and stepparents who do this well.

The potential negative effects upon adult children of divorce lie squarely in the hands of the adults around them. It's not your fault. The decision to divorce is difficult for all those involved, and the decision to then remarry carries its own fears and burdens. When parents are caught up in their own happiness, newfound love, and hopes for the future, they can sometimes forget that the process for their children may not be so smooth and simple. Awareness and prevention are key factors in achieving success in remarriage and stepparenting. Children of divorce do not just get swept along with the tide of newfound love. You were not as lonely as your parents for companionship and reconnection. You still had two parents who already had plenty of logistical complications to contend with. Sure, you wanted your parents to be happy, but just because your parent fell in love with this new person and their five children didn't necessarily mean that you and your sibling would, too. Everyone needed to work together to achieve positive and long-lasting results.

The feelings, needs, and reactions of a child of divorce during remarriage are important considerations. They are somewhat generalized and, at the same time, they are unique and individualized. No one is saying that parents should not remarry or have significant relationships. If that were the case, then they would be teaching you a different and probably negative lesson. They would only teach you about independence and the ability to be comfortable and happy alone and not in a relationship. Your parent's remarriage can bring harmony and a sense of completeness to you, your siblings, and your own family. We hope that your parents and stepparents were or are thoughtful, kind, aware, patient, sensitive, good negotiators, willing to compromise, good at balancing their own needs with yours, nonjudgmental, and that they have enough self-knowledge to make the decision to remarry from a heartfelt but well-informed and thoughtful position. If this was not entirely the case, we hope chapter 9 will give you some useful ideas so that you can go forward to forge healthy relationships.

PART II

Recovering from Divorce: Building New Relationship Skills

Chapter 6

Taking Care of Yourself

How long has it been since your parents divorced? The years have gone by and time has passed. You're an adult. Do you feel like you have become one of the grown-ups you looked at when you were a child? Or do you still feel like a child yourself? Do you feel that even though your parents divorced those many years ago and have gone on with their lives, the divorce is still affecting *you*? If "time heals all wounds," when will enough time have passed?

Focus and Attitude

Healing and recovery take more than time. Leaving a wound or injury to just heal on its own is often far less than sufficient. It used to be thought that after a heart attack, the best treatment was to have the person rest. Patients would, in essence, give up most of what was important to them and sit the remainder of their lives resting so as not to stress the heart. However, in the last twenty or more years, people are rarely so disabled by such an injury to their heart. With appropriate medical supervision, they are up and around as quickly as possible. Many times the person is actually exercising more *after* the heart attack than before. Many times people report feeling stronger and healthier after their cardiac rehabilitation. They did not just let time take its course. Rather, they became focused in a healthy way on their heart and changed their attitude about illness, diet, exercise, and so on. This led to their bouncing back and achieving resilience in response to the stress of the heart attack.

As we have seen throughout the first half of this book, divorce is a different type of stress, but nevertheless a major stress on the child. When parents, friends, and other concerned individuals wait for enough time to pass for the child to adjust, they are not fully providing what is needed to help the child cope with that stress. But, that time has passed. It's no longer up to others to help you bounce back and adjust. If you wait for Mom or Dad to say or do the right thing, understand, or apologize, you are still giving them control and power over your life in the present. Your adjustment to their divorce is more likely dependent on your willingness to focus on your own responsibility towards healthy adjustment. It can no longer be about your parents' attitude. It is time for healthy change because you have decided you're ready. It is now time for you to make your happiness dependent upon you, not them.

Making Yourself a Victim

Many adult children of divorce focus extensively on what happened to them during childhood. It's a focus on the external world and how that world has been cruel, unfair, or unsupportive. Such an external focus puts you in the role of the victim, and it keeps you there. It's a way of thinking that ignores your own strengths and the options you can take to lead a healthier and more enjoyable and enriched life. It creates negative expectations of yourself, others, and relationships. In short, an external focus creates illusions that seem very real.

★ *Self-Fulfilling Prophecy*

When Bill's parents divorced, he discovered that his mother had another relationship. This upset him greatly, especially as Bill's father often editorialized about Bill's mother. Bill heard over and over how awful his mother was, how his father was pained, and how his mother (and women in general) just couldn't be trusted. As an adult, Bill's significant other, Mary, often canceled their plans because of the demands of her job. Over time, Bill became quite anxious and then convinced that Mary was not truly interested in him. Her statements to the contrary did little to decrease his anxiety. They argued over whether she was interested in someone else. Bill was often angry and jealous. After a time Mary ended the relationship. Bill is now even more convinced that he was right. Yet, Mary actually called it quits because she couldn't tolerate Bill's chronic jealousy and doubts.

★

In this example, Bill needed to take more internal control and separate his current relationship from his past experiences. If he was disappointed when Mary canceled their dates, he needed to discuss this with her without making jealous inferences. It would have been more productive to shift his attitude away from "what she is doing to me" and toward recognizing that he indeed had options about his attitude and behavior toward Mary. Mary's behavior may have emotionally replicated the issues around the divorce for Bill, but it did not have the same meaning in reality.

Attitude is about looking at how we perceive the events that we experience. While our perceptions may seem correct and involuntary, they indeed can be changed by our questioning their accuracy and rationality. Things are often *not* the way they seem to us. Our past experiences color our perceptions, as a fun-house mirror distorts our view of ourselves.

Bill may have had to talk himself through it by saying, "Even though I wonder if Mary is interested in someone else, I am just not going to go there. She says she cares a lot about me. She seems really interested in me when we're together. I'm just not going to accept that she's interested in someone else until she tells me so. I'll take the chance. Mary and I are not Mom and Dad. I need to not question her to death. Instead, I'm going to pay attention to enjoying the time we have together." As Bill learns to change his attitude and focus in a healthy way on his relationships, his feelings change and his behavior also changes. This then leads to a difference in the quality of his time with his romantic partner.

Resilience

Attitude and focus are only two ingredients in the process of taking care of yourself. A somewhat new but very important concept in the divorce literature is that of *resilience,* or the ability to spring back from negative events. When medical professionals, families, and patients did not recognize that people could be resilient and bounce back from their heart attack, the patients sat and waited to grow old. However, when there was recognition that people could indeed recover, the focus then switched to helping people not just view themselves as victims, but rather to actively work at recovering and living a fulfilling life.

Resilience does not just apply to medical conditions. Children and adults are remarkably resilient in dealing with life's stresses and trauma. It is not that these events don't affect us. Rather, it's a question of effectively coping with and managing the stresses that we experience so that they do not rule our lives. You don't have to view yourself as permanently damaged by your parents' divorce. You *can* bounce back.

One fifty-year-old man described his parents' divorce as a monster that he had to fight with on a daily basis. "It ruled my life," he said. "It was like I always had to be on guard for how it was going to get me each day. I had to fight to keep it from ruling me. I had to fight with my parents, my wife, and my friends to not let what happened to me as a child happen to me again as an adult." He went on to say, "I then realized that the divorce happened over forty years ago. I realized that when I stopped fighting, I stopped giving it power over me. I just needed to be myself and live my own life. I needed to accept people for who they were and not try to make things perfect in my current relationships." This was a crucially important insight. When we stop seeing ourselves as victims, we do not have to fight and refight the old battles. This then can allow us to pay attention to living more normally in the present. We can be resilient by allowing ourselves to let go of clinging to the divorce, its pain, and our sense of being a victim for all eternity.

Letting Go of the Pain

The emotional pain of your parents' divorce is well-known to you. It's probably with you often. In fact, the more you think about it, the more it bothers you. There are constant reminders of divorce. It can seem like the word "divorce" is present all around us. Pick up a newspaper, turn on the television, talk to a friend. Who is getting divorced now? Who is having an impossible divorce? You might even hear from your own child, "Jill's mom and dad are getting divorced. How can they do that to her?" There may be constant reminders of your parents' divorce as you plan for family gatherings, listen to one parent still talk negatively about the other, and so on, and it's really easy to relate all of these events to your own pain. You can keep that pain in front of you always. You can view yourself as a "victim," "survivor," or "adult child of divorce." These labels can then become your primary identity and keep you focused on the guilt, anger, and grief associated with the loss of your intact family.

As an alternative, you can focus on what you *did* get from your family and childhood. You can remember the love you received from one or both of your parents. You can pay attention to how that love was shown. You can think about what positive life lessons your parents taught you. Did they teach you how to deal with Billy the Bully or Mary the Meaney? Did they tell you they were proud of you? How did they support and nurture you? What did they give you besides a divorce?

Journal Exercise 6.1

You might want to take a moment or two and actually write down the positive life lessons you learned from your parents. Feel free to use the space below or your journal to clarify some of your thoughts. Some positive life lessons my parents taught me:

1.

2.

3.

4.

5.

A healthy childhood is not just about having two parents who stay married. There are so many terribly dysfunctional intact households. Rather, it seems that a major factor contributing to a healthy childhood is how the child is made to feel about themselves. Did you feel loved, valued, or cared about?

Journal Exercise 6.2

In the space below or in your journal, please take a moment to jot down some positive feelings that one or both of your parents had about you.

1.

2.

3.

4.

5.

Was childhood all negative for you, or did you get some positive communications from your parents? Does it help to spend your energy on the pain and the negative, or does it feel a bit better to think about the positives? You cannot totally ignore the negatives, but it's likely that they're getting far too much airtime and crowding out your memories of other important feelings and events that also played a part in shaping your personality.

Remember though, your personality is not just shaped by the positive and negative events of your past. It is also shaped by how you view yourself in the present.

Reducing Guilt

Children often feel that they are the center of the universe. Infants have little understanding that there is anything else besides being hungry, wet, or tired. They may be aware of their parents and perhaps a sibling, but there is little sense that there is anything else than the moment at hand. As children grow, they begin to see that there are other people who have a place in the world. A toddler learns to share and wait their turn. A first grader learns to be polite. Teenagers start to learn that other people have feelings, too (a hard lesson for some). But all of these skills take effort because children have a difficult time seeing that the world does not revolve around them. When parents divorce, many children therefore believe it may be their fault.

★ A Clean Room Making the Difference

Melissa was seven years old when her parents split up. On Friday night her parents (who had already decided to divorce but hadn't discussed it with her yet) scolded her for keeping her room a mess. On Saturday morning they sat her down after breakfast and calmly told her they were getting divorced. What did Melissa think? Well, to her it seemed perfectly likely that her messy room was to blame for the split. Melissa's parents continued with the divorce. It wasn't a high-conflict divorce, but her parents were still caught up in the disentanglement of their marriage. They were loving to Melissa, but no one stopped to realize that she was blaming herself for the divorce. To an adult it seems preposterous that Melissa could possibly think her parents were getting divorced because her room was messy. To Melissa, it made perfect sense. She said to herself, "Yesterday, my parents got mad 'cause my room was dirty and then my parents told me they were getting divorced." These two things happened close in time to one another and Melissa knew how important she was to her parents and their happiness. If they are unhappy enough to get a divorce, she felt it must in some way be related to a failing in her. Melissa grew up and didn't even remember that night she was scolded for her messy room. However, the feelings of somehow being responsible for her parents' divorce remained.

★

Even in adolescence, children of divorce can feel responsible for their parents' decision. They often look for a reason, and with the heightened self-focus of adolescence, look to themselves.

★ Was It His Fault?

Fourteen-year-old Tim was very upset that his parents were getting a divorce. He was distressed that they were unhappy in their marriage and that they were going to be breaking up his intact family. When Dad suddenly moved out, Tim became "the man of the house." He was uncomfortable in that role. He saw how sad Mom looked and how money was tight. He thought, "If Mom and Dad were back together, things would be better." When visiting his dad he would tell him how sad Mom was. He would get angry at Dad saying, "How could you do this to Mom and our family?" Tim would think, "If I was sick, maybe they would at least come together to take care of me." He would hear his parents say that they still cared about each other and would see them occasionally go out to a restaurant and he would think, "There must be something I can do to fix this and get Mom and Dad back together." But Tim's wishes never materialized. His parents divorced. Tim grew up always feeling bad about himself. He was very successful in college and in his career, but always felt that no matter what he achieved, it wasn't good enough. There was a nagging feeling that he was "bad" and no matter what he accomplished, the feeling did not go away.

★

Guilt is a useful emotion when it helps us make choices that are in line with our values. However, for kids who feel responsible for their parents' divorce, the guilt and resulting low self-esteem aren't productive. These children hold onto bad feelings and are negatively impacted by them for years, well into adulthood. Both Melissa and Tim felt as if they were responsible for their parents' divorce, because they believed it was up to them to have prevented the divorce. As adults, they clearly could have seen otherwise, but they never spent the time to challenge the deeply held belief that the split was their fault. They were so used to blaming themselves that they automatically believed it. They both needed to let themselves off the hook and clearly recognize that they had nothing to do with their parents' divorce.

Divorce and marital reconciliation are adult decisions. They cannot possibly be related to the behavior of the child. Even if your behavior as a child was mean, rude, or otherwise inappropriate, you did not cause your parents' divorce or fail when they did not reconcile. This concept needs to be absorbed and integrated into your thinking. Children cannot control their parents' behavior (even if we, as children, would like to).

Anger Management and Forgiveness

So, if it was not your fault, whose was it? The field of possible suspects shrinks quickly until you narrow it down to Mom, Dad, or both. When children of divorce recognize this, they can also realize that they hold (or have held) a significant amount of anger toward their parent(s). This anger can fuel ongoing relationship problems with parents and other significant people in your life. The anger can make it feel as if the divorce occurred yesterday. You might have very little tolerance for any mistakes or flaws your parents may have. It may be that you also hold them to a much higher standard than you hold virtually anyone else. If so, you may find that you're frequently angry over new issues that arise as they fail over and over again to meet your expectations.

Therefore, one step to helping limit these negative feelings in your life is to make your expectations of your parents the same as they would be for most people. By recognizing your parents' humanity you can set your expectations of them in a manner that is more akin to their actual strengths and weaknesses. This can keep you from being as disappointed and angry. You're lowering the bar to a more realistic place where you do not hold onto the childhood illusion of your parents being all-knowing and always right. You are recognizing that they're just ordinary people with their own baggage and histories who did the best they could (even if it didn't always seem good enough) to get through life with its demands, confusion, and disappointments.

Another strategy is to see your parents as they are now. How old are they today? In your mind's eye, do you still see them as you did when you were a child or do you see them as being more like their true chronological age? How long ago was the divorce? How long do you need to carry the anger? You can punish your parents for the rest of their lives, but you will suffer an even greater loss. It's important to give yourself and them a chance to live in the present and recognize that you don't have to punish them (and in turn yourself) with a life sentence for the "crime" of getting divorced.

Moving beyond the anger is not pretending that nothing happened. It isn't simply forgetting about the pain. Rather, it is acknowledging the pain but also acknowledging that the time you have today is precious and that there are other elements to your life and relationships besides endlessly concentrating on the divorce of years ago.

Letting Go of the Survivor Mentality

Often anger is also connected to the sense of how your life has been changed by the divorce. Do you view yourself as an adult child of divorce or as a "survivor" or even as a "victim" as you relate the divorce to your childhood and current struggles? This can then attach the old anger to situations and other people in the present. It can center your day-to-day focus and your identity on the divorce and keep you feeling as powerless now as you did as a child. When you say, "If it wasn't for the divorce, then . . ." you are making the divorce responsible for your unhappiness. This inevitably distracts you from the responsibility and power you now can have over your daily decisions and your own happiness.

Journal Exercise 6.3

In the space below or in your journal please list three major ways your parents' divorce has affected (and still is affecting) your life:

1.

2.

3.

Think of the situation where two older adults are diagnosed with a terminal disease. In fact, for the sake of the example, let's have them diagnosed with the same illness on the same day. They each have the same symptoms, prognoses, and expected life spans. One emotionally collapses, sees their life as over, and essentially waits to die. The other decides to live as full a life as possible during the time that remains. What do you think is the difference in the quality of their last days, weeks, months, or years?

Unlike the example above, divorce is not a terminal disease. It is a major stressor but it doesn't have to ruin your life. In fact, divorce is not even about your whole life. Think back to your child-hood. Regardless of your parents' divorce, your childhood probably included some positive experiences. Consider them and take a moment to list a few of them below or in your journal.

Journal Exercise 6.4

Positive childhood experiences:

1.

2.

3.

It is important not to make the divorce the center of your child-hood or the center of your current adult identity. It was one impor-tant event or series of events, but the divorce is not you. It may have played a part in shaping your experiences, but you are far more than your parents' divorce. Your are not simply a "victim" or "survivor" or "adult child of divorce." You are a whole person with heart, soul, compassion, values, strengths, and weaknesses whose parents hap-pened to get divorced. As you recognize your full identity, you begin to take away some of the power of the divorce. You can make choices as an independent, free-thinking person, not as a victim or survivor. Divorce doesn't have to be the central element of your per-sonality. Your personality can be based on the full spectrum of who you are.

Self-Nurturance

As you fully recognize yourself as more than a child of divorce and as you let go of the focus on anger and guilt, you can begin concen-trating on taking care of yourself. Unfortunately, many children of divorce feel that taking care of themselves in a nurturing manner is selfish. They may have even been told as much as a child, having heard one or both parents say, "How can you just be thinking about yourself when we are going through this divorce? Who do you think you are?" Children who have been parentified have learned to be selfless, putting themselves last. Children in very dysfunctional families learn to disregard their wants or needs because they've learned they'll only be disappointed or worse.

A message is sent to many children that if you take care of yourself, you're doing something wrong. This is a very destructive message. Taking care of oneself is not necessarily at all selfish. There is an important distinction between self-nurturance and selfishness. Selfishness occurs when someone attends to their own needs without consideration for or respect of the position of others. This then causes the other person to be neglected (and usually hurt) in the interpersonal transaction. A very basic example of selfishness would be taking the last piece of pizza because you are still hungry, without asking the person you are with if they are still hungry. Selflessness would be leaving the restaurant hungry because you did not communicate to the other person that you were still hungry. A self-nurturing approach would be to offer to split the last piece or even order more so that neither of you go hungry. In other words, you would find a solution to the problem without disregarding the other person or yourself. That's right—you would not disregard yourself.

The key to self-nurturing is to recognize that you are part of the equation. You don't have to neglect yourself or be selfish. Recognizing and trying to address your own needs in a healthy fashion is what is important here. Will you always be successful and happy? Well, probably not. But you will be more empowered to address your needs and avoid being a victim unnecessarily.

Building Self-Esteem

When parents take care of their children in a healthy fashion, the children get the sense that they're worth being taken care of. They understand that they are lovable and of value to their parents. They hold onto this concept into adulthood, developing a sense of self-worth and healthy self-esteem.

If your parents' divorce limited your ability to have these experiences, then you are left with little choice but to build this sense of self on your own. You may look to others to give you what your parents did not, but in all likelihood this will not fill the void, since it is still seeking the nurturance from outside yourself. It needs to come from a more internalized sense of self, a sense that you are worthwhile, even if the world is cruel, ignoring you, or just doesn't understand.

Self-esteem comes from recognizing that each of us has inherent value, the same value a child feels in a healthy relationship with their parents. The child may do something that their parents do not approve of, but the child's value and the parents' love for the child never changes. This inherent value is what needs to be recognized in adulthood, especially if it was not cultivated when you were a child. Your value was and is inherent in who you were the day you were born, as it is with all children. It is not based on your achievements, the love you were shown, or how many diplomas or awards you have received. Your value is based on the uniqueness of who you are as an individual. It may seem too simple or silly, but Mr. Rogers (yes, *the* Mr. Rogers) was right when he would let kids know "You are special. There's no one quite like you. You are special just because you're you."

It's time to recognize that, in spite of your challenges and disappointments, you indeed have a specialness to you. You are the one who needs to take care of the person you are and give yourself the same compassion, support, tolerance, and encouragement you would give others, especially someone you care about.

By taking care of yourself, you limit the impact of the divorce. Your parents' divorce is not and should not be the center of your identity. You can allow the radiance of your personality to develop as you go forward through adulthood and touch the lives of others.

Chapter 7

Healing the Relationships with Your Parents

How long ago did your parent divorce? Ten, twenty, thirty, or more years? Does it feel like yesterday? Or does it feel as if your parents' divorce continues to be almost a daily factor in your life? How angry are you at them and how resentful do you feel about the years of hurt and disappointment? Does it feel as if it will always be this way? It doesn't have to. You do not have to bear the burden of their divorce as a legacy throughout your adulthood. You may now have children of your own who could benefit from healthy relationships with their grandparents. You may notice that your parents are aging. Perhaps it's time to look at how you can improve your relationship with one or both of your parents rather than feel that the divorce of years ago is still playing a major role in your life.

As a child, you learned about what it meant to be divorced through the eyes of a child and the words and actions of your parents. Your views were first shaped by the normal ways a child thinks and views their world. For example, it's likely you felt the divorce was your fault. Or, you may have said to yourself, "I'm so angry at Mom and Dad. I just wish they would stop fighting," or "I would do anything if they would just get back together." If the marriage was more hostile or violent, you may have been particularly angry with the more aggressive parent. It's possible all of these years later that anger and the associated disrespect has continued. You may have found countless examples of the flaws of one or both of your parents that keep fueling the anger and the distance between you and them.

Similarly, your views were also shaped by their behavior. Back then, your parents may have been twenty years or more younger than they are now. They were going through one of the most stressful experiences of their lives. They may have been depressed, frightened, and heavily burdened. Finances may have been incredibly tight. They may have felt public embarrassment and humiliation. In short, they may have been upset and distracted, naive, and not adept at dealing with this major stressor. Unfortunately, you may have not been able to get the best that they had to offer.

Now they and you are much older and hopefully wiser. However, if you're stuck in the anger and the hurt, you cannot begin to take advantage of the wisdom that may have developed over the last many years and the love that may have always been there, even if it was hard to see. The anger and hurt needs to be dealt with if the relationship is going to have a chance to grow anew.

★ *Now or Later?*

Janis grew up hating her mother who, when Janis was fifteen years old, divorced her father. It was a difficult divorce, and Janis missed her father terribly. He traveled for work, and she rarely saw him during the week. Every other weekend was barely enough. Janis blamed her mother for this major loss and felt disdain for her mother at almost every turn. Their life together was difficult at best. Janis was strong willed and rebellious, and she and her mother argued frequently as Janis was determined not only to assert her independence, but to have her mother pay for the divorce.

Janis moved out of her mother's house when she went to college. Things slowly began to improve after that point. She was able to see her father more, and her relationship with her mother became less intense. Over the next twenty-five years, Janis's relationship with her mother actually began to improve and solidify. Her relationship with her father also remained strong.

Now, at fifty years old, Janis said, "I'm so thankful for the last twenty-five years. I now have a mother (and my daughter has a grand-mother) who is truly a friend. Overall, if I have a choice, it's more important to have a close bond with my mother throughout my adult-hood than to have had a close bond throughout my childhood."

This close bond did not occur by luck, magic, or just by allowing time to pass. It grew out of hard work and Janis' dedication to building and sustaining loving relationships with both her parents. Janis worked with each of her parents to salvage both relationships, in spite of the pain and hurt and the many years that had passed.

★

You *can* decide that you want to try to improve your relation-ship(s) with your parent(s). Of course, your commitment is only one half of the equation. Your parent(s) will also need to be committed to the same process. Either way, you can still try to deal with some of your issues with your parents. In the sections that follow, we discuss a process by which you can first address some of your issues with your parents and then (if you are both committed) begin to heal your relationship. Even if you do not get the commitment from your par-ent(s) to heal, you may be able to benefit from effectively addressing your issues.

Addressing Your Issues

The issues around your parents' divorce are likely to be complex. You may have many competing feelings and concerns. There may be layers upon layers of anger and hurt that have to be addressed, as there can be a history of repeated hurts even long after the divorce has been finalized. Many adults seek to speak to their parents about the divorce, but are unprepared (as are the parents) for this very important interaction. The following guidelines will give you a sound process for approaching your parent(s).

Decide on Issues and Questions in Advance

Many times children confront their parents in the spur of the moment. You may be in a restaurant, at a family function, under the

influence of alcohol, or angry about something that has recently tran-
spired. You may be confused by the flood of emotions that you feel
in the heat of the moment. Rather than respond to the impulse to
speak to or confront your parents at that time, we recommend that
you thoughtfully decide in advance what are the most important
issues and questions that you want to address. Discussing these
issues with one or both of your parents is very important. You certainly would be prepared for a far less crucial business meeting. This
interaction with your parent(s) may be the only instance for quite
some time when you will have their attention focused in this way, so
you also need to be focused and prepared. You might want to think
about your questions from the following perspectives. We have
included some samples to help you consider what's important.

- *Questions that clarify facts:* How long were you having marital problems before you decided to divorce? Whose decision
  was it to get divorced? Why did I see one parent so little? Is
  it true that you didn't want to see me that much?

- *Questions that clarify motivation:* Why did you decide to move
  so far away from me? Did you get divorced knowing that
  you were going to hurt me? Why did you not show up at
  my school or athletic events? Why did you not regularly pay
  child support, but went on vacations with your new hus-
  band/wife?

- *Questions that clarify the parent's feelings in the past:* What did
  it feel like for you to get divorced? What did it feel like
  when I wasn't with you? Why did you hate Mom/Dad?
  What was it like to think about getting divorced back then?

- *Questions that clarify the parent's current feelings:* How do you
  feel about what happened to me as a result of your divorce?
  How do you feel about our relationship over these many
  years? What would you like our relationship to be like now
  that the divorce is so far behind us?

You can, of course, have many other questions that are pertinent to
your own experience and concerns. Think about them carefully and
decide which ones are most important to you. These need to be the
focus questions for any dialogue you may have with your parent(s).

Decide What You Want to Accomplish

It's crucial that you are clear about the purpose of discussing the past, your feelings, or the future. Generally, there are a few common goals that most people have for such an interaction. For example, you could focus on simply having a forum to voice your opinions, thoughts, and feelings about the impact of the divorce. This approach can be useful to say what simply needs to be said. We refer to this goal as "planting the flag."

When we first landed on the moon, we planted a flag. Who would see this flag? Were we claiming the moon as property of the United States? Hardly. We were instead affirming our presence and the significance of the actions that had taken place. This was important unto itself, even if planting the flag didn't produce other results. Similarly, you may find it helpful to *calmly* make the comments to your parent(s) that need to be made simply to give yourself a voice. Perhaps you would be saying what you needed to say years ago when you were a child. Nevertheless, you would be planting the flag simply by expressing yourself. The advantage of this approach is that you're not setting yourself up for more disappointment. All you are asking your parent(s) to do is to simply listen. You just need to say what is on your mind, which is significant in its own right.

On the other hand, you may be looking for an apology or some recognition and sorrow from your parent(s). This is a bit trickier and puts you in a more vulnerable position. Parents have varying degrees of capacity to apologize (even years later). They have their own defensiveness, narcissism, and personality issues. If you are looking for an apology, it's probably best to go ahead and ask for it. You can even say to your parent(s) that you are not looking for them to justify what happened around the divorce. Rather, you want them to recognize its negative elements and the major impact that it had on you.

Finally, your goal may be to create a forum by which you can have more discussions and begin a process of rebuilding the relationship. You may want to aim at reaching the point where you and your parent(s) can meet regularly. For example, some adult children who live reasonably close to their parents will set a time and place to get together on a regular basis (the mall, a bowling alley, a restaurant). They will use this bit of structure to start a small routine that gives them time to be together, talk about many things, and in some way get to know each other as they are now, instead of as they remember or expect each other to be.

Sometimes you may not fully know what it is you want to accomplish at the outset. You may simply want to start by planting the flag. You can then evaluate your parent's response and see if you want to take additional steps. There is no rush or time pressure. It is, however, important to remember that your parent may be just as fearful about being vulnerable with you as you are with them.

Decide on Your Approach Strategy

The planning for your first meeting is very important. In general, this meeting should be held in a conducive location such as a neutral, quiet place without a lot of distraction. You should not be under the influence of alcohol. There are a number of decisions you can make that can help you feel more comfortable and in control. For example, you can decide on the following:

- *Type of first communication:* Most people think that such a discussion has to be face-to-face. While this can often be quite valuable because of the nonverbal communication that occurs, there are times when it is easier to first communicate by mail, telephone, or e-mail. Sometimes the lack of face-to-face contact can help both people feel less intimidated. Mail and e-mail can allow both of you to chose your words carefully and thoughtfully. It can also allow you to review what was said. This way, you're making sure you are accurately sending your communication and accurately receiving the communication of your parent(s).

- *Time of the meeting:* If you're meeting face-to-face, you should have the meeting when it's good for you. You should be rested and prepared. It is best to not be pressured by time commitments to others or by activities or work. Leave yourself plenty of time (hours may be needed) so that you don't have to rush to relieve a baby-sitter, get back to work, or satisfy some other commitment.

- *Location of the meeting:* If you expect the meeting could get volatile, it's often better to have it in a public place that can serve to keep voices quiet and even offer witnesses, if needed.

- *Who should attend:* Often, a first meeting is best conducted solely between you and your parent. If you are at odds with both parents, you might best schedule to meet with them separately. You don't want them to replay the dynamics of their marriage and divorce. You might also find it best to first meet with the parent who is most supportive or closer to you. This can be good practice for your meeting with the other parent. Additionally, if either of you bring someone else, it's likely that you or your parent will feel attacked and outnumbered. Sometimes siblings decide to meet with a parent together. Even in this case, the parent can feel ganged-up on and become more defensive. In some families, the relationship of each sibling to the parent is quite different. You might not even be aware of those differences, but they can negatively impact the process during this very important meeting.

- *Your attitude during the meeting:* You attitude should be calm and direct. This is not a time to bash your parent. Rather, it's an opportunity to try to get some understanding or closure on the past and possibly set the groundwork for the future. The more appropriate your behavior is, the more likely it is that even if the meeting goes poorly, you will be comfortable with your own actions. Furthermore, if your behavior is not hostile, your parent might be more likely to respond in a more honest and positive fashion.

- *What you will do after the meeting:* Even if you have left yourself plenty of time, you should plan what will happen after the meeting. Ideally, you should plan to be with someone who can be supportive of you. You may want to plan for some quiet time. The meeting should not occur before a major work or family obligation. We can be fairly certain that if your parent meeting went poorly, you will not be at your best later in the day. Be good to yourself and take care not to set yourself up to be overwhelmed after the meeting.

Decide What You Want to Say

It can be very helpful to think carefully about the words you want to use in this discussion. It's best to communicate clearly and carefully. You don't want the discussion to go off course by having more misunderstandings. While you cannot be in control of what your parent says, you can be sure that you are communicating accurately. Sometimes, it can be useful to role-play the central points you want to communicate in advance with a significant other or therapist.

Prepare Your Parent for the Meeting

It is as important for your parent to be prepared for the meeting as it is for you. While the "sneak attack" may be emotionally gratifying to consider, it rarely seems to pay off. Generally, the parent feels quite threatened and will either attack back or get defensive. This generally perpetuates the dynamics of the past and can again leave you feeling hurt and frustrated. Instead, it's important to give your parent time to think about the meeting. They should have a chance to think about the past and what they want to say to you. Simply put, you can tell them you would like to get together alone to talk about your questions and feelings and their thoughts about the divorce. This gives them a chance to not feel ambushed, to prepare for this very important discussion, and hopefully to respond as best they can.

Prepare Yourself for What You Might Hear

While it is unlikely that you can be able to predict exactly everything you'll hear at the meeting, you can nevertheless make some guesses about what your parent might say in response to your questions and concerns. Think in advance of two or three responses you might hear and what your best reactions might be. You might be surprised to find that you are then better prepared to respond to them. The point here is that a bit of mental preparation and rehearsal can go a long way to dealing with the possible surprises of parental guilt, anger, tears, and new information that is disclosed to you.

In short, take control and responsibility to design this interaction. Treat the meeting and discussion with the respect and importance you deserve.

Talking about Anger and Resentment

Conventional wisdom and pop psychology tell us to "Let out your feelings. Let them know just how bad you feel." Yet, many times this advice leads to a torrent of rage from both people and even more pain. At other times there can be a resounding thud when there is little positive outcome or response from the parent. Many of our clients tell us, "I don't want to just relive the past," and this is often a good impulse. If you express the anger and the resentment you felt from your childhood in the manner of a child, your parent will likely act as "the parent" and not as another adult. You will not feel like an adult yourself and may just repeat the old parent/child cycle from years ago. Expressing your feelings about the past needs to be different than reliving them in the present.

Some people actually find it helpful to think about the expression of past feelings as if they are almost talking about someone else's feelings. They speak calmly and rationally about what they felt in the past, rather than stirring up all the emotion of the past in the current interaction. They speak as if they are an adult who is speaking for a child. As a matter of fact, in any interaction you now have with your parents, you *are* an adult. You're no longer a child, and they no longer have the same parental influence over you, unless you give it to them. The goal for the expression of your anger and resentment should be to communicate this information to your parents in a way that they can hear. Be careful to guard against talking down to them, making condescending remarks, or whining. It is also crucially important that, regardless of your parent's response, you leave the exchange with respect for yourself. Maintaining your dignity is important. If you feel your parents do not respect you, be extra vigilant to make sure you don't give them more ammunition. Their respect for how you handled the discussion is not as important as your respect for your own actions and the way you interacted with them. Psychotherapy (individually or in a group) can help you sort through your feelings and look at options for effective communication with your parents.

It's also important to know when to *stop* expressing your feelings. One of our colleagues said it quite well as, "It's important to know when to go into the pool and when to get out of it." There are times when you may need to stop the discussion about emotions (perhaps because it is either too overwhelming or it's no longer productive) and move on to another discussion that is lighter or even superficial. You don't have to stay in the emotional pool until you feel like you're drowning. Get out when you need to and before you are emotionally exhausted.

Overcoming Parent Alienation

By far, this can be one of the most difficult challenges for you to face. How can you possibly work to rebuild a relationship with a parent whom you may hate, disrespect, see as incredibly flawed, whom you don't trust, and whom you hardly saw at all? You may not even be aware that parent alienation is present. For example, you might say, "I wasn't alienated. I don't like my mother/father for good reason. Look at all they did and look at what they didn't do. I may be their child legally, but that's where it ends." But even if you don't see it as out-and-out alienation, the anger and distance still take their toll. You and your children won't have the chance to benefit from any positive experiences with this parent as you all get older. You miss the opportunity to heal and to get to know your parent as the person they are now, at this time in their life. It's possible (even if it seems like a remote possibility) that they have matured a bit and can see the value in interacting with you in a manner different from what you experienced as a child. They too have had years to reflect on the past. They are in a different place in their life and may now be ready to have a healthier relationship with you. Imagine if it was possible and beneficial but neither you nor your parent took the first step. You would never know what you'd lost.

So, what's the first step? It's actually saying to yourself that you are willing to take the risk that you will indeed be hurt or let down once (or many times) again. The risk is investing in a process (not an *outcome*) that will either confirm all that you know is wrong with that parent or may show you that they have some worthwhile traits. The risk is letting go of the pictures of them that you fully believe are true and instead taking a chance that you only know them as they were through your eyes of long ago. Your parent will, of course, have to take the same risk. You cannot be responsible for their willingness or lack of willingness to look at rebuilding the relationship. You can only focus on your role and options.

For example, you could approach this parent, saying in writing, by phone, or in person that you want to set up a brief time to talk. They may or may not be receptive. They may blame you for letting the years go by. They may not show up for the meeting, telling you it's your fault because you gave them the wrong time or place. They may show up for the meeting but be blameful of your other parent, angry, or belligerent. All of this is outside of your control and not your responsibility. You can only decide if you're willing to take the risk to begin a dialogue.

You may be prepared for your parent to act in a condescending, uncaring, or hostile manner. This may fit the patterns you have experienced and expect. You can say, "Oh well. Just as I thought," and move on with the knowledge that this parent indeed is not yet ready to try to work on the relationship.

A scarier prospect can be that of finding the parent remorseful and eager to begin communicating with you. This can lead to a great deal of uncertainty, as you do not have much of a history interacting with this parent in such a manner. Can you trust these behaviors? You probably won't at the outset, or even after quite some time. Yet, you can decide to move forward regardless of the distrust, evaluating your progress as you go.

The Bond and Understanding

The process of moving forward may feel like walking blindfolded through a strange but vaguely familiar house. You might be saying, "Now where are those stairs?" as at any moment you expect to fall headlong down into the basement. It's important to at least recognize that, even if it's negative, there is a unique and probably untapped bond that connects you (and your children) with the alienated parent. This bond is what leads to the anger, hostility, and disrespect. Many adult children will say, "I don't care about my parent. I've been hurt too badly and too much time has gone by." Yet, often it seems that they are saying, "I've been hurt so badly, because I have cared. I wish I wouldn't care so that it would just stop hurting." The bond is what leads to the hurt. If there truly was no bond, you probably wouldn't be affected by the actions of this parent. The slights and emotional assaults you've received over the years from people to whom you are truly unattached probably have far less impact on you than when you think about being vulnerable with the parent from whom you're alienated.

This bond can be the bridge from the pain of the past to the possibility of having a better relationship in the present. That better relationship needs to first be based upon an attempt at understanding. The points made at the outset of this chapter about a first communication with a parent apply doubly in the case of the alienated parent/child relationship. Here also, the first step can be to try to build an understanding (even if not an agreement) about the past and its impact. This understanding should be based on both of you learning about the impact of the past on *each* of you. That's right— you need to learn about the impact of the past on your parent as well. You probably won't agree with your parent's perception or justification for their actions, but you need to hear their views, as they need to hear yours. You may be surprised to hear how their experience of the divorce and other stresses led them to behave in a manner such that you felt so disregarded. This does not justify what they did, it just puts it in a context.

Building on the Bond

There is probably little that your parent can now do to make up for the hurt and disappointment of the past. That opportunity is long gone. If you look to have the old pain go away, you're probably going to be disappointed yet again. The question as we see it is, "Can I have at least the semblance of some type of reasonable relationship with my parent at this point in time?" This is not likely going to be the parent/child relationship of the century—certainly not at the start, if ever. It's almost as if you are getting to know this person for the first time now. A younger adult is getting to know an older adult, and vice-versa. These two adults happened to have shared a past, but there has been a tremendous amount of time and hurt since then. The challenge becomes one of seeing the kind of relationship that can be constructed in the present.

Yet, as we said earlier in this chapter, the key here is to avoid slipping into the role of a young child. You are an adult and need to approach the interactions with your parent as such. You don't have to allow yourself to be intimidated or taken in by your parent. You also don't have to rage at them or teach them a lesson. Get to know this parent as they are today. Do they still seem to be the awful person they were back then? Or do they seem older and markedly less intimidating? If you met this person as a stranger at a bus station, would you be intimidated? Would this person be very threatening? Actually, at this point in your life, what power do they really hold over you? You can simply begin to get to know this older adult as they are now and then make your own decisions about the level of a relationship that would be beneficial for you and your children. Remember, you're no longer trapped or a victim. You are an individual unto yourself and no longer a young child trying to live through an impossible divorce.

Dealing with the Aligned Parent—A Special Circumstance

When you talk to your alienated parent, do you feel as if you are being disloyal to your other parent? Do you feel guilty about having dinner with your alienated parent and not your aligned parent? How would your aligned parent feel if you build a neutral or even a positive relationship with your alienated parent? If these, or similar nagging questions cause some level of tension in you, it is quite possible that some attention needs to be paid to your relationship with your aligned parent.

As you begin to explore developing a relationship with your alienated parent, you may find that this rekindles some of the old childhood issues with your aligned parent. That parent might feel quite anxious about the possibility of you becoming close to the alienated parent. They may be concerned that you are about to "switch sides" or that you will hear about all of their faults from the alienated parent. Your aligned parent may appear sad and as if they are losing you or your love. They may even go as far as saying to you that they can't understand how you would want to see the other parent after all these years and that they feel that you're hurting them by seeking out the other parent.

It's easy as an adult to have a recurrence of the same family dynamics that may have been present long ago. Yet, the difference is that now you may be able to see the process more objectively and clearly. This objectivity can help you avoid falling into the same roles as when you were a child.

As an adult, you should be free to have a relationship with each of your parents. That relationship may vary from one parent to the other and, as the years pass, you may find that the relationships between you and each one of your parents change. Yet, the freedom to have the relationships is truly one of your rights. Furthermore, the relationship with one parent should not impinge on the relationship between you and the other parent. In a sense, there should be a firewall between those relationships. Your relationship with your mother and father are each equally valid, even if one of these relationships is more satisfying, supportive, or healthy than the other.

Some of the concepts above may be necessary to discuss with the parent with whom you are more closely aligned. Additionally, you can tell the parent who might feel as if they are going to lose your love that no matter what you hear from the alienated parent and no matter what your relationship with the alienated parent becomes, there is plenty of love to go around. You, of course, have enough love for both parents. If they had stayed married in a healthy, intact family, you would love them both and they would not feel threatened by that. In fact, they would likely encourage it and feel upset if you didn't love the other parent. Their feelings toward each other and their marital status does not change the fact that they both are your parents and that you can have feelings for each of them that are separate and different than their feelings for each other.

At other times, the aligned parent can voice a concern that you could be emotionally hurt by exploring the possibility of building a relationship with the alienated parent. You might hear, "Your [father/mother] was so awful to you all these years. What makes you think they won't be now? You're just setting yourself up to get hurt again. I love you, and I just don't want to see you hurt again. I mean, look what your [father/mother] did to me in the divorce. Don't you see what they're capable of? I don't want that to happen to you."

This parent needs to hear that you are fully aware of the emotional risks that you're taking and are appreciative of their concern. Nevertheless, you have decided to begin on the course you have plotted and hope that you can at least count on their love and emotional support, even if they think that you are being foolhardy.

You may also notice that if the parent with whom you are well aligned pushes too hard, you might begin to feel a sense of anger toward them. This anger may also be a hint about underlying anger from years ago. Many times children caught in parent alienation dynamics actually can become quite enraged by the actions of the aligned parent. You might, for example, begin to think that the aligned parent manipulated you to keep you away from the alienated parent. You might feel that the aligned parent deprived you of your right to have a continuous and viable relationship with your other parent. If this begins to occur, it's important to try to avoid setting up a ricochet process where you simply switch from being alienated from one parent to being alienated from the other. It is important in these circumstances to work on dealing with your anger toward the aligned parent, as well. At these times, a brief course of joint counseling can be helpful so a facilitator can help you and your aligned parent discuss and resolve the salient issues that have arisen.

Avoiding Today's Loyalty Conflicts

Unfortunately, family systems don't have some type of natural law that dictates an end to loyalty conflicts when you reach eighteen years of age. In fact, intact families also wrestle with loyalty conflicts. They struggle as they try to arrange Thanksgiving dinners when both families are close enough to see (but not together), when they deal with two family obligations that occur on the same weekend, or when they have to sit down at a family church or synagogue service. Who will sit with whom? Who should be with each subsection of the family? Yes, adult children in intact families face many of the same demands.

However, the demands you face are compounded by the fact that there are even more segments of a family system that may have expectations from or make demands on you.

★ *Is It Us or Them?*

Paul and Stacey have two children, aged twelve (Jessica) and fifteen (Chris). They are wonderfully active and vital children involved in a number of extracurricular weekend activities. Paul's parents divorced many years ago and have since remarried other people. One weekend Jessica had a soccer game at 10 A.M. on the town field. Chris had basketball tryouts at 10:30 A.M. at the high school gym. Jessica also had a birthday party to go to in the afternoon, and Chris wanted to have a friend visit. To complicate matters, on this otherwise "routine" weekend, it was also Paul's stepmother's birthday. Paul and Stacey planned to drop by for an hour or two later in the afternoon when they took Chris's friend home and picked up Jessica from the party.

As they were about to leave the house for Jessica's game, Paul's mother called and said to Stacey that she and her husband wanted to drop by in the afternoon and maybe have an early dinner. Stacey burst into tears. "It's all too much," she said. "I just can't do it anymore. How can I make all of this work? There's just too much going on. Can't we just have a life of our own?"

Stacey was caught in the middle of trying to please everyone and yet feeling like she could not please anyone. She didn't feel like she could tell Paul's mother that they couldn't see her because it was Paul's stepmother's birthday. This would give her mother-in-law the impression that Paul's stepmother was more important. Yet, at the same time, she couldn't tell Paul's father that they were going to pass on his wife's birthday because Paul's mom was coming over. Then, of course, there were the children's feelings to consider. They had plans that didn't quite include hanging around the house with their grandparents. In a matter of moments, Stacey hit overload, wanting to just run out of town by herself to avoid trying to please everyone.

★

Balancing all of these competing needs is far from easy, but there are a few guidelines we can offer. Remember however that these are general recommendations that probably will not produce amazing results on any one occasion. Rather, they are guidelines for repeated use over time.

Schedule, Schedule, Schedule

Advance planning is crucial in the family that has a complex lifestyle or family constellation. Spur-of-the-moment plans are often likely to backfire. Kids, adults, and grandparents need to have their expectations set in advance. Last-minute changes are likely to lead to conflicts and hurt feelings. Your extended family, as well as your children, can learn over time that they need to try to avoid last-minute planning. Plan well in advance and give the schedule to everyone.

Clearly Communicate the Specifics

The expression, "The devil is in the details" is clearly relevant when you're trying to deal with coordinating and being responsive to multiple schedules and needs. Families of divorce have many combinations of individuals who can be present at a family function. There are far too many opportunities for miscommunication. Specific information should be communicated clearly and promptly whenever possible and not left vague. You should not think or hear, "Well I just thought you would *know* that . . ." Be clear and specific to all parties. When expectations are not met, many people can unnecessarily feel that they were intentionally slighted for "the other side." If you're doing the planning, be clear and specific.

Set Precedents

As time goes by, people can adjust to most routines. Just as you had to adjust to routines as a child, you can now set routines in terms of how you spend time with each of your parents. For example, you don't have to figure out Thanksgiving anew each year. As an adult, you can set the pattern for how you will spend Thanksgiving and let everyone involved know the plan in advance. You don't need a court order. You're the one who can determine what you will be doing. You can start to set expectations by becoming somewhat predictable, letting your parents know what to expect of you from one situation to the next. This consistency will make it less likely that your behavior will be interpreted as a statement of loyalty toward one parent or the other.

Maintain Limits and Boundaries

At times you'll need to be firm when dealing with your parents, extended family, and even your stepparents. You will need to make it clear that your feelings toward each parent are different than their feelings toward one another and that you are going to have the relationship(s) you seek rather than the relationship(s) they would have. For instance, imagine planning your wedding. Your parents are divorced, and your father and mother are both remarried. In fact, your mother has remarried a second time. Your first stepfather was married to your mother during most of your childhood, as your parents divorced when you were rather young. You feel connected to your parents, your stepmother, and *both* your stepfathers. You also feel connected to their parents. Is this a mess? Who do they want you to invite to the wedding? Who will sit with whom? Who will walk down the aisle? Should this be your worry? Or, should you simply invite those people *you* want at your wedding and tell them you are inviting the people who are important to you based on your relationship with each of them—not based on whether they like or dislike each other? At times you will have to make it quite clear that your decisions are yours to make and not based on every one else's needs or wants.

Expect to Disappoint

If your parents are sensitive to loyalty issues, you need to expect that you can't and won't please them all of the time. You cannot force them to be comfortable with your decisions and never feel hurt or insulted or disregarded. This happens even when married children from families without divorce make choices about which in-laws they see. You need to be careful not to make your parents' feelings your responsibility. You can tell them that you regret that they feel bad and hope they understand your decision, but you cannot make them approve of your actions or stop acting in a way that seems guilt inducing. On the other hand, you need to take the pressure off of yourself to be the perfect child who never makes anyone feel bad.

In summary, you are entitled to the opportunity to have healthy relationships with both of your parents. Building these relationships will take both time and work on all of your parts. You need to remember that you can only be in control of your own part of the interaction and cannot shape your parents into being who you would like them to be or to act the way you would like them to behave. Similarly, they cannot shape you to be or act the way they want you to. As an adult, you don't have to always please them or seek their approval. You can, however, get to know each other as you are now and strive to build an adult relationship that has the bonds of history, pain, and love.

Chapter 8

Guidelines for Healthy Nonromantic Relationships

Your parents' divorce has tentacles. Whether or not you approve, it has its effect upon many different aspects of your life. Even when you don't want it to be there, it can rear its head to intrude upon your day-to-day relationships and decisions about how you choose to lead your life. Do not begin to think that you've completely escaped the fallout. That can be a marvelous use of denial and avoidance, but what would Freud have to say about it? Your parents' divorce is your legacy and the more aware you are of the causes, process, and results, the more you can minimize its negative impact on your own life going forward.

Good and Bad

The relationship fallout from your parents' divorce can be either positive or negative. Sometimes children are witness to very high-conflict relationships or even those that are just constantly irritating and unhappy. Perhaps you lived in a state of agitation and had few models for loving, caring, and well-balanced marriages. If this was the case, you may not know what to look for in your own relationships and may have few definitive criteria from which to evaluate the men and women who come into your life.

Conversely, the end of your parents' marriage may have led to a cessation of the fighting and maybe even a better working relationship between your parents. Perhaps they were more successful parents apart than they were as a married couple. If you fit into this category, you experienced the healthy result of a difficult decision. You learned that changes may have had to be made for the opportunity to have a positive future, and you may have had the chance to see your parents function as independent individuals. If you're lucky, you may also have had the chance to watch your parents negotiate their new world and establish healthier bonds with people who support and nurture them.

Unfortunately, the negative side often outweighs the positives of your parents' divorce. The leftover conflict and the effects of all the years of your parents' marital struggles may have left you with many unresolved issues about many different relationships in your own life and little ability to resolve them. Please note, we are talking here about *all* the different kinds of relationships you encounter, not just the ones which lead to romance and perhaps marriage. Your parents' divorce can affect your work life, your friendships, your extended family, and even relationships with your acquaintances. All of these relationships may be affected by the very same issues that may abound in your love life. They are not exempt.

In this chapter we will examine some of the relationship concerns that may impact your nonromantic relationships. We will save the discussion of your love life for the next chapter. There is, of course, much overlap between the two. The hope is to broaden your concept of the effects of your parents' divorce upon your relationship life so as not to see these issues as isolated to the domain of the intimate relationship.

Boundaries

The concept of boundaries in any relationship implies demarcations and definitions that allow us to function together safely and securely. Boundaries provide a parameter for a relationship, a fence, a border, and a common ground. Boundaries provide clarity and comfort so that the relationship can grow within the established confines. The problem comes when boundaries are not well-defined. They can then become too fluid and flexible so that the relationship can become confusing and nebulous. Boundaries can also become too rigid so that a relationship may not have room to develop its own identity or to change over time. Children of divorce can distort relationships in either direction and have to be careful to be aware of these boundary issues. After all, your own relationship boundaries with your conflicting parents may have been quite distorted and lacking of adult definition and protection. You may, for example, have been exposed to adults who may have overstepped their roles as parents. Perhaps you became their confidants and not just their children. Or instead, you may have been "protected" from your parents' divorce by being kept in the dark and told only what they thought you needed to know. If this was the case, their manner was probably restrained and explanations were sparse. Boundaries were made of high walls, and you were left to your own devices to decipher their divorce and its impact on your life.

Now you're asked to establish appropriate boundaries in multiple relationships in your life. Where do you learn how to do this successfully? Our parents are our best models but can also be our worst teachers. Observations of others, their parents, their partners, and helpful feedback from friends, family, coworkers, and therapists can help to reeducate you and retrain you in setting the correct boundary lines in all the important relationships in your life.

There are, however, some common factors with regard to boundaries that may be helpful as you think about some of your relationships. These factors might best be illustrated by routinely asking yourself some important questions than can fit almost any relationship.

- *Type and purpose of the relationship:* What kind of relationship is this? Is it a business relationship, acquaintance, friendship, or family relationship?

- *Appropriate roles:* What are the expectations of each person in the relationship? Is there a protective role expected of one or both people?

- *Risks and level of trust:* How much intimacy and vulnerability should there be in this relationship and especially at this stage of the relationship? What signs do I have that it's prudent to risk emotionally or otherwise? How much should I risk at this point in the relationship?

- *Appropriate sharing of closeness and intimacy:* Is this a relationship in which I am truly comfortable being emotionally and/or physically close or intimate? Is there a pressure for the intimacy coming from within myself or from the other person? Am I ready for and comfortable with the closeness?

These boundary questions can pertain to any kind of relationship. You might want to rewrite these questions in your journal so that you can easily find and review them at different points in your current and future relationships. You might find them to be helpful guideposts as you journey through relationships.

Trust

The world of an adult child of divorce is based upon having experienced major ruptures in trust. At some point, the expectation that your parents and your family would last as a cohesive unit was destroyed forever. You knew that promises were made and then they were broken. That is not what your parents taught you to expect. Now you are told you're supposed to trust other relationships in your life to be loyal, helpful, and dedicated. Why should you believe this? Most of the things and people that you learned to depend upon changed. You may have moved, changed schools, houses, friends, and pets. You may have acquired new siblings and new stepparents. Your parents' financial situation may have been drastically altered. Your "stay-at-home" parent may have returned to work. You may not have participated in all of your chosen activities or gone to social events on weekends. Your parents may have even cared for you so differently that food, homework, discipline, and bedtime were not the same in both homes. Finally, your stressed-out, depressed parents may also have not enforced their own structure consistently even within their own homes. Nothing much in your world stayed the same, and you lost the experience of comfort that sameness brings. Obviously, your weariness and mistrust is predictable and probably self-protective. The problem is that it can get you into trouble.

There are a number of ways that problems of placing trust in others can display themselves in your behavior. See if you can find yourself in the following descriptions.

Changers

One way to deal with disruptions in trust is not to stay in any one place for too long. Then you don't have to worry about trusting anyone or anything because you have not allowed yourself time to build trust. Changers have built-in time limits in their relationships, places, and jobs. They usually leave and go on to other pastures when they feel that a trusting commitment is required. A move to action is seen as the best solution rather than to work on the fears behind the issue. Short-term trust is okay, but long-term trust is far too risky.

Clingers

For those of you who fit this category, trust may look like it's not an issue for you. Oh, but it is! At first glance, you appear to invest in relationships easily. The problem is, you stick like Velcro and sometimes exhaust even the best of friends. You are constantly evaluating your relationships with others, dissecting every little morsel, and never letting go. You appear needy beyond the interdependence appropriate in most relationships and cannot recognize when enough is enough. Others feel that your clinginess is suffocating. These clutching attachments stem from desperation and fear of loss. You're not sure that you can truly trust any relationship, and you know that you cannot tolerate the end of a job, friendship, and so on, so you fight with all your might not to let it go. In essence, Clingers keep a tight leash on their relationships, afraid that the relationship will end if they let go and just allow it to grow on its own.

Sabotagers

Those of you who fit this bill try to make sure that you are in charge of all the relationships in your life by sabotaging them before you can be hurt or rejected. You find things wrong, mess things up, come late to work, forget appointments and dates, and generally create many reasons why others cannot trust you. This self-fulfilling prophecy works very well. You can convince yourself that others are unfair, unreasonable, or intolerant. If you cannot trust others to be there for you, then you can make sure that you don't have to try them out for too long or be too trusting or vulnerable.

Distancers

For some, it's a lot easier to not even try. The solution here is quite simple. Don't bother to commit to anything too much. Keep your distance. In that way, you never have to feel hurt. At a distance, you can protect yourself by interacting with others only as needed. Distancers don't expect to trust beyond a certain degree. They don't admit they want or need anything more. The downside here is that you rarely have permanent relationships in your life, and the ones that you do have lack the level of intimacy that would heal your past hurts. What an ironic and unfortunate sacrifice.

Trust is something that should develop over time in relationships. Risks should be taken slowly and increase in vulnerability over time as the feelings of safety build. In a sense, building healthy relationships is like working for the CIA and gradually getting greater degrees of security clearance. As the trust develops in a relationship, you can gradually allow yourself to be more vulnerable.

Openness

The other side of the trust coin is your own ability to reveal yourself to others. Your capacity to be open to others has probably been damaged in much the same way that your trust was compromised. Even if you engage with others who are trustworthy and dependable, you may be hesitant to reveal yourself in ways that could leave you open to being hurt and rejected. It may, in the short run, feel better to be self-protective and careful than to take any risks. Unfortunately, because children of divorce often accept the blame for some if not most of their parents' divorce, the damage to self-esteem, self-confidence, and self-trust is significant. After all, if you view yourself as so powerful that your parents did not even remain married because of you, imagine how destructive you can be as an adult. Or, if you view yourself as so impotent that you couldn't even get your parents to stay together, then imagine how weak and ineffective you must be in the other relationships in your life. It may feel far better to wait, watch, and wonder than to reach out and take a chance on life. You may be so afraid that others will "find you out" that it just isn't worth it to engage at any real level.

Remember also that divorce itself, especially years ago, carried a very negative and shameful connotation. It may have occurred, but no one talked about it and the stigma attached to families of divorce was enormous. Hopefully in today's world there is a greater acceptance and understanding of divorce, blended families, and single-parent homes. Your parents' divorce probably reflected poorly upon you, too, and therefore you might not want others to know the truth, that you come from a "broken home."

Finally, the financial changes that may have occurred as a result of your parents' divorce might have left you feeling like you did not fit. Maybe you weren't able to go to the same places as the other children or have the same opportunities and sports and hobby equipment. Or maybe you had to go to a neighbor's or a baby-sitter after school because your mother went back to work outside the home, unlike the other children of that era. Or maybe one of your parents rapidly or totally exited from the marriage and your life, leaving you with a "parentectomy," again unlike most of your other friends. The anger and sadness were and are probably overwhelming at times. Maybe it's just easier not to show anyone your real feelings for fear that they'll burst forth without restraint and overwhelm someone else. Then they just might leave, too.

We have character descriptions in the area of openness, too. Try again to find yourself among these categories.

Hiders

These individuals believe that openness just isn't worth the risk. They may appear shy, but they are actually terrified to reveal themselves to others. The connection between vulnerability and rejection is too strong, and being alone and unconnected is better than getting hurt, or worse—being left.

Surfers

These people are very enjoyable to be with but not to love deeply. These individuals deal with their parents' divorce by acting as if it didn't matter. They take life as it is and make no emotional commitments beyond a certain level. They often look as if they are connecting, acting jovial, and engaging, but surfing the relationship world is their safest path.

Spillers

These individuals are quite the opposite side of the other two. They tell all and connect instantaneously, repeatedly placing themselves in the path of potential hurt. They don't have good judgment about to whom, when, and where to open up, and so they let it all hang out. Although they may have some chance of forming a relationship, they take the enormous risk that they have exposed themselves too soon or to the wrong persons. Their parents' divorce has left them without good self-esteem, a good sense of security, and good judgment about openness.

Self-Sabotagers

Unfortunately, these individuals will use anything to protect themselves from opening up to others. This includes self-destructive methods such as drugs, alcohol, anger, and abuse. They seek to avoid any real connection and don't want others to know them in any meaningful way. The potential pain of self-revelation needs to be covered up by substances or protected by volatile displays of anger and hostility. They successfully implement a self-fulfilling prophecy. Their parents' divorce may have left them feeling responsible and without recourse, and so they make sure that others stay away too. They make themselves toxic so others will reject them sooner rather than later.

As with trust, openness needs to develop slowly in relationships. Different types of relationships may call for different kinds of openness. For example, you might not discuss your salary with a friend or your marriage with your boss. Yet the reverse might be true, such that you might conceivably discuss your marriage with a friend and, of course, your salary with your boss. You can decide how open you will be and along what dimensions the openness will occur in your different relationships. It does not have to be one size fits all.

Conflict Resolution

All healthy and unhealthy relationships have their share of conflict, which is a natural part of working, living, playing, and loving other people. Adult children of divorce can have a particularly difficult time figuring out how to settle disputes with others. This spans all kinds of relationships, both inside and outside of your immediate family. After all, you were probably privy to all sorts of conflict before and after the divorce. Furthermore, you probably saw conflict go unresolved and spread into a huge conflagration that overtook your life and that of others whom you love. A belief can then develop that conflict is bad, should be avoided at all costs, and is unending. On the other hand, adult children of divorce can become so used to conflict that they can grow up with much the same conflict addiction that overwhelmed their parents many years earlier. Some of these children of divorce may feel that they have to "win at all costs" and find it extremely difficult to give in, accommodate, or say "I'm sorry" when in a dispute.

Adult children of divorce also often don't have adequate role models to teach them how to argue, disagree, and yet find a common resolution. They may routinely be exposed to the type of disagreements that only result in a stalemate instead of in resolution. Conflicts that are self-fueling and without conclusion are a matter of course. The focus on winning overtakes the need to find a solution. You may have too often experienced your parents not finding an agreeable middle ground or compromising with one another. Many parents who divorced were poor teachers and poor examples of how to resolve conflict. How could you learn these skills?

Again, see if you can find yourself in the following descriptions of conflict-resolution styles among adult children of divorce.

Aggressors

These individuals are argumentative about most anything! Most of their lives feel like a challenge, and much of their energy is devoted to winning battles. They are touchy, easily ignited, and hold little regard for the feelings of others. They have little capacity for empathy and therefore little ability to understand the varying positions of those around them. These adult children of divorce learned their lessons from the masters and view conflict as a constant war to be engaged in and won at all costs.

Agitators

These individuals are not quite at the extreme of the aggressors, but they cannot live without creating a relatively constant level of agitation. They, too, are used to living in conflict without resolution. They needle others, examine opinions inside and out, take too much time to solve problems, and heat things up just for the sake of creating a reaction. The extreme discomfort that this creates for those within their families and in other relationships in their lives is a source of familiarity for them.

Capitulators and Compromisers

These individuals are very good at figuring out what it will take to end conflict quickly. Unfortunately, they do this by routinely giving in and giving up. They are easy individuals with whom to resolve conflict because they're all too willing to compromise or to let the other person prevail. Their own opinions just do not matter enough. In fact, they are not really very adept at truly resolving conflict, but instead very adept at determining how to calm the potential storm. They often lose their own identities in the process. These adult children of divorce learned well how to grab the fire extinguisher and put out the flames before they get too hot to handle.

Avoiders

These individuals dance away from virtually all conflict and avoid it if at all possible. Unlike the Compromisers and Capitulators, Avoiders try to disengage from any and all forms of disagreement before it even starts. They are passive with a capital "P" and do not voice strong opinions or even formulate them in the first place. They can be either far too dependent or far too independent in their behavior with others. This allows them to be taken over by others without resistance or to take off when the going appears to be getting too conflictual. These adult children of divorce learned well how to avoid the conflict they lived with all their lives and may still even be living with well into their adulthood.

The Last Straws

These adults first react as Avoiders. They run from conflict and are often passive in their interactions with others until they cannot stand it anymore. Then they may overreact, shifting to becoming Aggressors. This can lead to confusion and volatility in their relationships, as well as feelings of guilt when they go too far.

Conflict resolution does not have one simple formula. There are times when it is certainly advantageous to give in and avoid a fight and yet other times when you should "go to the wall." The trick is being able to pick and choose which approach is best for the situation. Furthermore, conflict resolution can occur by partnering with the other person rather than just going to war. Sometimes a softer approach actually works better than using a hostile or intimidating manner. You can think carefully as you face conflict about when and how to react and avoid the instinct to react impulsively based on your past experiences.

Your Working World

You might be asking how your parents' divorce could have anything in the world to do with you and your work environment. Well, it does. Boundaries and opportunities for conflict are everywhere and are especially important in your relationships with fellow workers, supervisors, managers, and those whom you manage. Relationships in the working world require clarity of position and an ability to communicate effectively both up and down the chain of command. Feedback in the form of one-on-one meetings with your supervisor or full surveys of your coworkers, and meetings with consultants, are all very common in today's companies. It's often very hard for employees and employers to establish good working relationships that maintain professional boundaries, resolve conflict, and allow for some degree of comfort and intimacy. Adult children of divorce can become confused by the signals, sometimes stepping way beyond the lines and becoming too personal or being too reticent to interact and being perceived as distant and unmotivated.

For instance, parentified children of divorce may not respect the boundaries between themselves and their bosses. If you learned early on that there is little difference between you and your parents in place and responsibilities then you may misperceive your position in your working environment and blur the roles. This can work in both directions and may manifest itself by your being too familiar, offering advice and suggestions out of proportion to your status, or taking charge and not working as a team player. For female adult children of divorce who have not had adequate male figures to relate to safely and consistently, the whole male/female interaction in the working world can feel disconcerting. Working relationships can be contaminated by a need to be liked and not just to be competent. Others may misread your cues, perhaps even causing you to experience sexual harassment. At times you may find that you feel taken advantage of by others. Awareness is a key point. It's important to remain very conscious of your actions at work and how they may be viewed by coworkers.

Here are some helpful guidelines to direct you through the maze of workplace relationships.

Secure a Clear Job Definition

Make sure that you know exactly what your job entails before you start. Ask the necessary questions and get the answers. Don't just read the job description, but use your interview to paint a clear picture. Talk to others at your level about their experience.

Communicate with Your Managers and Employees

Consistent feedback is the best preventative medicine for boundary problems at work. Check things out. Ask how you are doing and frequently clarify the boundaries expected in your job.

Keep Home and Work Separate

Your personal life belongs outside of the office. This may seem like a simple concept, but as an adult child of divorce you may have had your life infected by your parents' unending conflict. Intruding phone calls, letters, legal involvements, gossip, and more defined your days without regard to your needs. Perhaps voice-mail messages and e-mails flooded your world without rules or respect. Don't repeat the pattern. Work time is for *work*. You need to teach others in your life that there are other times and places for personal issues to be discussed.

Learn How to Be a Team Player

Children of divorce may either seek to self-protect or they may instead be overly involved in taking charge of a project or meeting. Learn your place. Learn to delegate. Learn to listen. Learn to use the resources around you. Trusting others to work with you honestly and effectively may be hard for you, but can bring volumes of rewards.

Resolve Conflict Efficiently

This is surely a hard one for adult children of divorce. If you were caught in the tornado of your parents' conflict addiction, then you probably have little ability to know how to negotiate workplace disagreements or even greater conflicts. This may take some retraining. Use your available resources. These include your human resources department, Employee Assistance Program, other mental-health practitioners, and formal and informal mentors. They all have a lot to offer. Watch and listen to others who seem to be good at resolving conflict and observe yourself carefully. You may have been used to communications that perpetuated conflict rather than those that were aimed toward decision making, resolution, problem solving, and effective implementation.

Friends and Family

Boundaries, openness, trust, and other issues in relationships with extended family, stepfamilies, and friends are also impacted by the same factors as are our work and love relationships. These relationships can easily be contaminated by old concerns, old experiences, and old behaviors. All that old learning is hard to break. These archaic patterns may create a number of roles that repeat themselves in so many areas of your life. See if you can identify yourself as we examine some of the characteristic personas worn by adult children of divorce.

The Ultimate Caregiver

Many children of divorce are placed in unnecessarily adult roles. The absence of one parent creates logistical needs, and children, especially older children, are called to action. Parents sometimes work long hours and children are asked to fend for themselves and their siblings. Parents sometimes form overly adult relationships with their children, discussing topics such as finances, dating, and other adult issues usually reserved for the other spouse.

The positive result of this caregiver practice is that you become a conscientious parent yourself, are a good and caring friend, and know how to handle the basics of running your life and that of others efficiently and effectively. The negative result is, of course, that you may grab control that is not yours, become overwhelmed with all you "have" to do, and may not recognize that others need to learn responsibility as well as you.

Some of the steps that you can take to free yourself of the caregiver role are:

- *Set realistic goals every day:* Keep your daily to-do list short, and complete only those things that you set out to do. Don't let others unnecessarily add to your agenda without regard for your needs and desires. Some adult children of divorce, especially women, act as if they are rubber bands. These rubber bands expand and expand and expand beyond the length that anyone ever imagined. Watch out, or they will pop!

- *Take good care of yourself:* Try to do something just for you every day and at least one larger thing every week. This can be something like exercise, reading, massage, lunch with a friend, or just sitting quietly for fifteen minutes. Adult children of divorce often feel guilty about focusing on themselves. The needs of others *can* wait while you reasonably take care of yourself.

- *Let others take care of you:* Believe it or not, others may want to do things to take care of you, too. Sometimes this is spontaneous, but you may have to give them the opportunity every once in a while by asking for what you want, even if it's only a cup of tea. Your strong, take-charge selflessness can convey a misperception that you don't need anything at all. Do not be afraid to show your vulnerability or ask for help.

The Self-Protective Turtle

Some adult children of divorce are too afraid to allow themselves to need or be needed by others in any reliable and consistent manner. You avoid what others crave. You don't expect others to count on anything from you, nor will they be allowed to give to you in any meaningful fashion. Maybe you will show up on time for Sunday dinner. Maybe you will remember your sibling's birthday. Maybe you will visit regularly at the nursing home. Or then again, maybe you won't! If no one expects anything from you, you can't disappoint them. And if you don't expect anything from them, *you* won't be disappointed, like you were so many times in the past.

There are ways to come out of your shell and form relationships with others in your more intimate world of friends and family.

- *Plan ahead and be realistic:* Avoid overcommitting. Don't just agree to plans when you know that you may not be able to make it. You may be scared to disappoint but you risk coming across as uncaring and untrustworthy. Give others reasonable expectations of how they can count on you. Sign up for activities, say yes to invitations—and go. Focus on the positive aspects of the event and do not give yourself any outs once the decision is made.

- *Listen and learn:* The best way to begin to form relationships or to cultivate already existing relationships is to listen and ask questions of others. In that way you show an interest in them and get to know them better at the same time. Watch out, though, because they may then want to get to know you. Take a risk and allow yourself to share some of yourself with them in return. You won't find a good fit with everyone, nor they with you, but that's only normal.

- *Remember that you have needs, too:* It's really true that "No man (or woman) is an island." You, too, have a need to be cared for, receive help, and accept nurturance from others. It may be hard for you, but let yourself out of that shell enough to enjoy the rewards of a relationship. The interdependency of a balanced give-and-take in different kinds of relationships is a wonderful and essentially human experience.

- *Speak your mind:* No one can get to know you or your opinion if you don't speak your mind assertively. The ability to trust in your own judgment may have been damaged, but your judgment itself may actually be sound. Take a chance that you may have something valuable to say and that others may listen.

- *Don't just give in:* People cannot engage with you if you're always the one to give in to others' opinions. Your own identity remains elusive and no one really knows who you are. That may be the idea behind your protective turtle approach, but you need to engage in a constructive dialogue and seek reasonable resolutions to conflicts or you will always be the passive victim.

Change Is in Your Power

As you go forth in your life and interact with others, you will need to be aware of the pitfalls and fallout of being an adult child of divorce. Always remember that you have the tools and power to change the course of your own life. The effects may be very real, but the implementation of healthy and constructive solutions is up to you. The behavioral patterns you learned in childhood *can* be changed if you focus on developing new and better ways of engaging in your work, family, and friend relationships. Yes, you may risk experiencing loss and the hurt and pain that goes along with each life occurrence, but risk management is certainly not what relationships are all about. Avoiding risk and vulnerability by protecting yourself or by blasting forth in relationships to reject others first or assure that they will reject you only leaves you lost and alone. These are familiar feelings for adult children of divorce, but the false security that staying on the periphery provides is not worth the real losses. Healthy relationships in your life can rebuild your world, yourself, your family, and your job or profession, as well as heal the wounds left behind by your parents' divorce. It takes a good dose of trust, a pinch of risk, a serving of self-awareness, and a good helping of desire to recover from the past.

Chapter 9

Taking Back Your Love Life

Now, what about love? In the realm of the heart, adult children of divorce often have a lot to learn. It's one thing to work on your relationships in all the other areas of your life, but romantic love is another thing altogether. You haven't had the best of role models, and maybe you don't have much faith in the concept of long-term commitment. If all you saw (and maybe continue to see) is conflict and hostility, you may decide that romantic, long-term relationships are just not worth it. In fact, some researchers (Willetts-Bloom and Nock 1992) have found that a child's perceptions of their parents' marital satisfaction is a key factor in determining the age at which the child (as an adult) desires to get married or start having children. This factor was even more significant than whether or not the parents were married or divorced.

On the other hand, you may yearn for all that you didn't see in your parents' relationship and maybe too readily jump into relationships that look or sound promising. Notwithstanding the importance of other areas, the ability to form lasting and committed love relationships is a primary concern for many adult children of divorce. Awareness, understanding, careful and thoughtful choices, and a keen desire to change behavior patterns or dynamics that damage interpersonal connections are all necessary to form a strong foundation for the development of healthy and permanent romantic relationships.

Where Do You Fit?

Let's begin looking at this sensitive and complex concept by first having you examine some of your thoughts and beliefs about romantic relationships. These concepts collectively can have a profound influence on your feelings about yourself, relationships with significant others, and your ease at being vulnerable. They can influence what you say and how you treat your significant other and the very fabric of the relationship.

Journal Exercise 9.1

Please answer the following questions here or in your journal to determine just where you fit on the relationship commitment scale. This exercise will help you answer the big question: "How hurt and scared am I?"

1. I believe that most relationships fail to work   Yes/No
   out successfully.

2. I believe that getting close to someone I love   Yes/No
   could potentially be hurtful and dangerous.

3. I believe that the best way to hold onto a   Yes/No
   relationship is to hold on tight.

4. I believe that my partner needs to prove that they   Yes/No
   really love me.

5. I believe that money equals power in relationships.   Yes/No

6. I believe that the best protection in a relationship   Yes/No
   is to be independent and responsible for myself.

7. I believe that avoiding conflict at almost any cost is Yes/No
   the way to keep relationships safe.

8. I have little idea about what a relationship should   Yes/No
   really be like.

9. I believe that I will most probably end up like   Yes/No
   my mom or my dad anyway.

10. I believe that waiting a very long time to get   Yes/No
    Imarried truly tests a relationship.

11. I don't like to need anyone, nor do I like anyone   Yes/No
    to need me too much.

12. No matter what I do, chances are that my   Yes/No
    relationships will never last in the long run.
    There is a strong possibility that divorce may
    be inevitable.

Now, look over the items you answered "yes" to. These items will likely give you clues to those fundamental belief patterns that may interfere with seeking to be open and to maintaining long-lasting relationships.

The statements in the exercise are all legitimate concerns of adult children of divorce. It's important to identify the areas that affect your relationships and address them directly so that you can establish new patterns of intimacy. One can understand your wariness to commit or your intense desire to jump into or stay in relationships that are not healthy for you. Only *you* can change that course and give yourself the opportunity for a full life, including a long-lasting love relationship.

Intimacy and Vulnerability

The fear factor in intimate relationships certainly stems from real-life experiences and from past history. That fear forms a set of cognitions, thoughts, or perceptions that then determine how you approach the love relationships in your life. Fear can have a paralyzing influence on your behavior. You may deal with the fear by steadfastly avoiding commitment, or you may react by vaulting headlong into relationships, hoping to overcome your anxiety by denial. Obviously, neither of these approaches is going to get you the results that you deserve—a lasting and committed successful relationship.

Journal Exercise 9.2

So just what are those fears anyway? Which of these fears do you experience? Put a checkmark next to the ones that ring true for you.

❑ *You will be left alone.* Adult children of divorce don't want to re-experience the loneliness they saw and lived through during their parents' divorce.

❑ *You will be a failure, so why try?* Adult children of divorce can protect themselves against their own fears by expecting the worst.

❑ *You will be a victim.* Your experience tells you that you have little control over your life and little ability to change the situations around you.

❑ *You are damaged goods.* Adult children of divorce can fear their parents' divorce is disfiguring and has marked them as being inferior.

❑ *You will hurt your own children.* You worry that your children are not safe from the contamination of the epidemic of divorce.

❑ *You will lose yourself if you let yourself need someone.* You fear that dependency results in a loss of your identity and sense of self and that it ultimately ends in rejection.

❑ *You will contaminate any relationship you have.* Since you have no idea what relationships should be like, you believe that you will somehow sabotage them every time.

The cognitive patterns that result from the above fears create a set of irrational beliefs that tend to take hold when a relationship threatens to materialize. These irrational beliefs are based on your childhood experiences and have a strong hold on how you approach new relationships, as well as how you evaluate relationships which have been ongoing. This set of beliefs is in place well before you even meet someone. In fact, the beliefs are doing their work on you even when you're unaware of them. The incorrect assumption is that these beliefs protect you in some way from the potential of experiencing hurt and disappointment—and maybe even your own divorce. In fact, they can do just the opposite. They can become a self-fulfilling prophecy if you let them have too much of your time and energy. They do not allow you to exercise your own good judgment, experience hope, or make changes. They drive you instead of you driving them.

⋆ *I Love Too Much*

Kirsten was twenty-five years old when she came in for counseling. She had just experienced the breakup of a fifteen-month relationship with Paul, and she was depressed. She had thought Paul was going to propose to her when he asked her out to dinner on Saturday night, but instead was "blown away" when he told her he wanted to break up. She had loved him with all her heart, barely went a moment without thinking of him, and had tried to anticipate his every wish. How could this have happened? How could Paul tell her he felt she loved him too much, that it was too much "work" to be in a relationship with her, and that he couldn't be himself? Kirsten was shocked and devastated.

Early on in counseling, Kirsten described her parents' divorce. They had divorced when she was nine years old. She lived primarily with her mother and saw her father (who was a pilot) infrequently when he was in town on the "right" weekend. Sometimes she would see him during the week for dinner. Kirsten described her relationship with her father as "incredibly strong and wonderful." She said, "The connection between us was amazing. We would both think of each other all the time. In fact, my father always had my picture taped in the cockpit of the plane, so he could be close to me when he was flying. Every time a plane flew overhead, I would know he was thinking of me. When I'd see him, he would always be sure to give me all of his spare change so I could call him and leave him a message anytime I wanted. I called him all the time, even though I knew he wouldn't be there or be able to call me back."

⋆

Your patterns may be as clear as Kirsten's. You meet someone and it can all go well for a time. You get to know each other, have fun together, and begin to become closer. You start to talk about your families, your hopes, and your past relationships. But, with the increased intimacy, along come your "friends"—the irrational fears. They are such an integral part of you that it can feel like you are lost and naked without them. They are familiar and can cause you to mistakenly believe that they provide a safety net that can stop you from falling down the deep abyss of intimacy and vulnerability. Yet instead of moving you toward a relationship, they surround you like a plastic cover and keep others from ever really touching you. What a way to live! You're surely bound to end up alone with this scenario, which will again just confirm the fear that you are not worthy, not good enough, or not lovable enough to be in a relationship anyway. "You see. I told you that relationships never work out for me!" becomes your litany.

Let's examine some of the dynamics in the kinds of relationships frequently developed by adult children of divorce.

I'm a Chameleon

Many adult children of divorce find it difficult to just be themselves. Children who experienced parentification may find it particularly difficult, as they often put their own needs second to those of their parents. Children who had to care for their younger siblings may also find it difficult to attend to their own needs. Certainly, if you in some way blame yourself for your parents' divorce and one parent leaving, you may think, "If only I'm everything they want, they won't leave." Unfortunately, this strategy can keep the "real you" from being present in the relationship. You can end up being "nice" but difficult to love, because the "real you" is not available as it hides behind the mask of the person you're trying to be.

Testing, Testing, Testing

The fear of loss can be so strong for the adult child of divorce that they may often test a relationship from every angle. Say that you meet someone and it looks like things are going along successfully. You may believe that you and your partner are falling in love. That becomes the time to put the relationship to the ultimate test. You begin to challenge everything. Like a true sleuth, you look under every rock and around every corner. You examine every little detail and query every loving statement. You look for the negative and focus less and less on the positive. You probe and poke at the relationship over and over again. You may, in essence, batter it with the force of a hurricane to see if it can withstand the assault. This testing can take many different forms.

- *Questioning:* You may test the relationship by continually asking your partner to tell you how they feel about you over and over and *over* again. You cannot get enough positive affirmation of their love because you have a hard time believing that anyone could *really* love you. It just doesn't compute or stick, so you have to hear it incessantly. If you pick a partner who has any trouble expressing their thoughts and feelings, the relationship won't last. Yet, even the most articulate and expressive of partners can get tired of this questioning game and give up trying to make you hear what you have trouble believing.

- *Prove it to me:* You may ask your partner to prove their love for you by engaging in a series of behaviors. In other words, you create a set of challenges—an obstacle course of love proofs. "When is the anniversary of our first date?" "Do I get a phone call every morning, noon, and night and all the times in-between?" "Prove to me that if you go out with coworkers, they are not more important to you than I am." The list goes on and on, but the point is that the challenges usually get more and more difficult to perform. There is usually no ceiling to the proofs and no finish line to the obstacle course. Inevitably, this process allows you to reject your partner at some point for failing the test, if they don't give up first.

- *Put up your dukes:* You're always ready for a good fight. You put relationships to the test by putting on the boxing gloves and coming out of your corner. Can your partner withstand the punches? Do they fight back or give up? You create conflict because that is what you know from your own background. You are all too familiar with fighting, but not very sure about resolution. Therefore, these fights can seem endless, rearing their ugly heads over and over again. Sometimes you don't fight fair, inviting your partner to hit back in the same way. Then you have an excuse to run in the other direction, out of the relationship and away from finding a way to settle your differences.

Why do you bother to do all this testing anyway? You're probably in search of the ideal partner who can meet your every need, know your every thought, and even predict your every move. You believe this person will know you so well that you'll finally get back all that your parents' divorce took away. This will be a love like no other before, and you will live happily ever after. All those love songs will be talking about you and your beloved, and all the poetry in the world will have been written about a love like yours. The problem here is that you may think that this is what you are seeking, but your actions make sure that true intimacy is impossible. No one, including you, could ever pass these tests; especially since they have no endpoint. Your expectations for the perfect partner and the perfect relationship can make certain that you avoid finding a relationship that lasts.

Never Say Never

Do you believe that love and lasting relationships will never come your way, or do you believe that you don't need anyone in your life because you can handle it all yourself anyway? The desire to avoid vulnerability and hurt is so strong that many adult children of divorce cannot let themselves love others with all that is necessary. They cannot open themselves up to real love for fear that they will once again be hurt and abandoned. Yet the irony of this is that what you want is not possible without risking hurt. No relationship comes with a map that avoids all pain and disappointment.

Your old wounds can be so deep that new hurts can quickly tap into the reservoir of self-protection, causing you to run in the opposite direction. This is especially true when you begin to rely on someone to meet your needs and to love you. Dependency can create a sense of panic, causing you to start looking frantically for what's wrong instead of all that might be valued. In essence, you can use your anxiety to make sure that you don't have to endure the possibility of abandonment. You may jump to leave the relationship first so that the other person cannot hurt you like your parents did one another or you. You may fear that if someone else leaves, you will be unable to go forward, so you make sure that you have control of the situation at all costs. Unfortunately, this can cost you the relationship. You can end up moving from relationship to relationship without commitment, often proclaiming that you do not need anyone permanent in your life, while, on a deeper level, you may feel lonely, scared, and disconnected. What a tall price to pay for what turns out to be pretty flimsy self-protection.

Adult children of divorce in this category can also assure that relationships remain "friends" instead of becoming more intimate partners. For some, second dates may be out of the question as you keep busy, busy, busy. Are you hard to reach and seem to have the most complicated schedule ever created? Are you everywhere and have little time to give to anyone? This assures that you can't even focus on a relationship long enough to determine if it even has a chance at a long-term involvement. Are you the quintessential volunteer? Are you the world's best friend? Are you a fabulous worker and involved in everything but a meaningful relationship? When all the busyness of the day is over and the lights go out, are you still really alone? You may be convinced that this is how it has to be, as you know you can never have a true relationship, but think again. It doesn't have to be this way.

Jumping In and Staying In

Some adult children of divorce react to their fear of intimacy with denial, moving headlong into relationships and clinging to them for dear life. You may hope to create a security blanket to undo the lack of safety you experienced from your parents' divorce. You may not evaluate relationships carefully enough and thus may overlook problems and signs of pending trouble. You may use intellectualization and rationalization to stay in the relationship rather than risk being alone. If you fear the possibility that you won't be able to find another intimate relationship, you may grab the first one that comes along and convince yourself that it is "good enough." After all, you may not even be sure what a "good" relationship looks or feels like. You can settle without realizing it, staying with the wrong relationship. Sometimes you might even stay in relationships that are destructive way beyond the point where someone else would most likely leave.

The power of having someone love you can be so strong that you will do almost anything to hold onto them. You will turn yourself inside out to please them and make the relationship work. You avoid conflict at all costs and subject yourself to a detailed process of self-examination if there are any points of difficulty. You believe that you don't have a choice but to stay, just like you didn't have a choice but to say yes in the first place. After all "you're *nobody* until somebody loves you." You can have a very hard time when you decide to make a change in a relationship because it feels like the old sense of childhood responsibility you felt for the demise of your parents' marriage. You are convinced that it will, of course, be *all* your fault if things don't work out. There are no other possible reasons. You feel sure that you must have done something terribly wrong to deserve to be treated like this, and consequently, you hold the key to make it right again.

Unfortunately, this is how adult children of divorce can remain in abusive or dysfunctional relationships. They don't think that they should leave, or deserve to, and cannot imagine being alone again. Something is better than nothing, and what you know is better than the unknown. Fear brings inertia and allows irrational thinking to predominate. "Things are not really so bad." "If I just try harder, they'll change." "I don't want to put my children through a divorce, so I'll stick it out." "No one else out there will really love me." It is the same old and tired thought patterns.

Another reason adult children of divorce don't leave is because they believe that they should take care of others. You may be drawn to those who need attention. Do others rely on you for most everything? You may know this role very well as you expand your parentified child role into your adult love relationships. Do you believe that if you leave you will be abandoning your partner, just as you felt you would abandon your parent if you tried to just be a child or to assert your developmentally appropriate level of independence in the outside world?

There is much cognitive work to be done in this area. You may find that it's hard to believe that your judgment is not impaired and that you *can* make your own decisions. It is also hard to take the risk that you might be alone again and feel lonely. "A bird in the hand" can feel like the least aversive and safest choice for you so that you're not left in the dust. It can seem that it is more important that somebody *(anybody)* loves you and wants to be with you forever.

The Multiples

Some adult children of divorce play the revolving-door game of multiple relationships to avoid the risk of intimacy. If this is your pattern, you may find that you change relationships like adolescent girls change their clothes. You never let a partner stay long enough to need them or develop any significant level of dependence upon them. That way, you don't have to feel the potential loss, and your heart can be seemingly protected from hurt and pain.

Unfortunately, you may not stay long enough in a relationship to make an accurate assessment of its true viability. Here, too, you can find fault where it may not exist and look for opportunities to go on to the next encounter as each person has some trait or characteristic that you just "can't" live with. You also may not be faithful to a relationship so you can have a convenient excuse to leave or to get yourself kicked out. When any relationship moves into the more difficult territory of closeness, you simply don't want to put the *work* in that it will require. You probably believe that relationships should come easily, and if they don't, you eject yourself as soon as possible.

Adult children of divorce who perpetually seek multiple relationships are usually addicted to the idea of *being* in love, rather than the idea that *staying* in love is the best part. You romanticize the relationship and expect it to stay at that ideal level forever. The feeling of being lost in the arms of another is utterly appealing, and you will do almost anything to be there. The early stages of a relationship can provide you with an opportunity to feel merged and connected. When this intense feeling begins to decline, you feel the need to bolt—before the infatuation anesthesia wears off. Relationships can be like drugs for you. The more the better, as your need to find new, different, and better ones predominate. What a terrible price to pay for the decisions of your parents and the failing of their marriage! If you constantly hop from relationship to relationship, you will never really know the joys of a real relationship where true commitment is the basic foundation.

It is likely that you have many questions about relationships and what to look for in a healthy relationship. Below are some guidelines to help you evaluate your relationships and the risks you are taking, using your good thinking, not just your heart or the legacy of your childhood.

Guidelines about Intimacy and Vulnerability

- *Be yourself:* The right person will love you as you are and for who you are, not for who you think they want you to be. They will love you with your strengths and weaknesses, your beauty marks and your warts.

- *Allow the relationship to develop:* Give the relationship time. You probably can't predict at the outset whether it will be the right relationship. You might be able to be sure that someone is not for you, but how can you truly know they are good for you from only one or two dates? Just like they don't really know you, you don't know them.

- *Risk slowly:* You don't have to share 100 percent of yourself, your history, your emotions, and your soul with a person on the first meeting. Take your time. You can risk slowly in a relationship, gradually taking greater emotional risks as you see that you can trust the other person in the relationship. Risk-taking does not have to be a sign of your devotion.

Rather, it should be more of a natural process based on the trust, comfort, and security that has developed as you have gotten to know each other.

- *Don't test the relationship:* If you're unsure of the other person's commitment to the relationship, it is perfectly all right to ask them. You don't have to construct a series of tests for them to pass. These tests can feel arbitrary and manipulative to the other person, who may actually lose comfort or trust in you. What an unfortunate occurrence it would be if you accidentally sabotaged the relationship by testing it.

- *Don't replay the past:* Live in the present. A significant relationship in the present will *not* undo the hurts of the past. You should not be the "child" in this relationship to make up for what you were not able to get as a child. Be the adult you are, and allow the relationship to develop on its own merits. Look for the relationship to address your adult needs, not the needs you had as a child.

- *Remember that you will get hurt:* This is not as negative as it might first seem. In almost any relationship, we can expect misunderstandings. We can expect that you and your significant other will be out of sync with one another on occasion. You may have different needs and different desires on a particular day or about a particular issue. You may accidentally step on each other's toes during the dance of life. You will feel (and probably dish out) emotional pain over the course of a relationship. It is not the presence or absence of pain that is the key, but rather how the pain is dealt with. Are there apologies? Do you both strive to allow the wound to heal? Do you both take care to avoid making the same mistakes over and over again?

- *Remember, you can't have closeness without vulnerability:* As difficult as it may be, it's crucial to a healthy relationship for each person to be vulnerable. The closer you get to each other, the more vulnerable each of you is to experiencing pain. If you always play it safe, you'll be keeping your distance in your relationships and miss the warmth, connection, and intimacy that can be uniquely marvelous.

Finances

While fear of intimacy and vulnerability are primary inhibitors to love relationships, money is also a very sensitive subject for many children of divorce, especially when it relates to their adult intimate relationships. It can represent the many different themes from the childhood issues discussed in the first section of this book. Money can start to represent how much you are loved. It may have become the way in which you extracted "love" from your parents as their guilt primed them to give material handouts. Both they and you could then confuse affection with buying material things. When you carry this over into adult relationships, you can find that money can symbolize love.

In the love relationships formed by adult children of divorce, money can also impact one's sense of power and intimacy in the relationship. You may begin to believe that if someone really, really loves you, then they'll get you what you need. If someone truly loves you, then they should show you that love by meeting your every financial or material desire. If they don't, then it must mean that you're not really worth it.

Do you remember during your parents' divorce and your years growing up in a divorced family how much money mattered? Was most of your life able to be assessed on a calculator and split according to some percentage between two parents? Instead of two parents jointly funding your activities, you may have had two parents who had to account to one another for every penny spent and for every financial request. Money may have been a continued link and commitment between your parents. Furthermore, the fact that child support is partially calculated on the time kids spend with each parent might have given you the impression that you, too, have a financial value, especially based on *where* you are rather than *who* you are. You can carry this concept into your adult relationships, valuing yourself and those you love in the very same terms.

When adult children of divorce grow up in households where money became scarce after a divorce, financial security becomes paramount. You may feel that safety in relationships can be achieved by earning enough not to need anybody to take care of you. You may have learned that people in relationships are valued by how well they can provide. You may have also learned that when people in relationships do not provide well enough it engenders intense anger and helplessness. You may think, "So why bother? I'll just earn it myself and keep my finances separate from my partner's. Separate bank accounts, separate accounting for expenses, separate credit cards, and separate economic lives will protect me just fine!" The problem here, of course, is that the separation of finances can be just another avoidance of full commitment to a relationship. Complete control over money can be a scary thing to relinquish, but is often crucial to establishing a truly interdependent relationship.

When adult children of divorce grow up in homes where they are exposed to parents who use money to continue to control one another and where one parent feels significantly financially disadvantaged, it may seem vitally important to earn, earn, earn. You may become a workaholic at the expense of balancing work with the need to nurture the intimate relationship in your life. The panic about not having enough and the need to protect yourself with financial security may drive you into working too many hours and focusing too much on work at the expense of your primary love relationship. In addition, you may feel that your value in a relationship is at least in large measure evaluated by how much you provide financially.

Money can become a convenient excuse for keeping your distance. You need to recognize its importance and the irrationality of the thinking behind your economic fears. Security is important, but a quest for financial security that is based upon a need to provide self-protection from old hurts, shame, and fear will be endless and unattainable.

You can use these guidelines to structure your thinking and approach about money and its impact on the power and equality in your relationships.

Guidelines about Finances

- *Balance your investment in earning money with your investment in the relationship:* So many people are concerned about their need for ever more dollars that they will do almost anything to earn more money or retain the opportunities they have to continue earning the same money. Yet, so often the relationship gets only a small fraction of the time, energy, and attention that one's job or career gets. Relationships need to be nurtured and can't always take a backseat to your job or career.

- *Share the wealth:* We strongly recommend that you consider unifying and not segregating your finances in a permanent long-term relationship. Prenuptial agreements and segregated accounts can set the expectation that the relationship will fail. We often wonder: if you are not comfortable risking your financial security in a relationship, how can you be comfortable taking the emotional risks to build a shared intimate relationship?

- *Share responsibilities and values around finances:* It should be clear that you generally have shared beliefs and values around money. You both don't have to produce the same income to share the responsibility for how your combined income is managed. Your parents' divorce may have taught you that money means power in a relationship. The confusion here is operating under a belief system that says that the amount of money produced is equal to the power one has in the relationship. Share the responsibilities, have shared values, and share the power, regardless of who earned how much of your income.

- *Seek honesty around money:* One key sign of a relationship that is in trouble is when one or both people feel they have to lie about money. Here again, if there is discomfort about who spent how much or who has how much, how can there be comfort in more personal, intimate, and vulnerable sharing? Dishonesty around financial matters may be a flashing neon sign that there is difficulty trusting or difficulty around having shared values about how money is spent. Both you and your partner should feel comfortable enough that you can trust each other implicitly about money (spending, saving, and talking about it).

Sexuality

The expression of intimacy through sexuality may seem especially scary for adult children of divorce. You may confuse sex with intimacy, or you may be afraid to give of yourself wholly in a physical relationship. You may be afraid of merging yourself with another for fear that the hurt of any potential loss will then be far too great. It's also so very easy to confuse the concept of sex with the very different concept of making love.

Some adult children of divorce form sexual relationships too fast and too soon. Sex becomes a means of pleasing others and yourself, as the pure physical pleasure becomes the main focus. The aim here is to feel good and make others feel good. This can lead to promiscuous behavior with multiple or sequential partners.

Maybe your parents were not good role models for the direct expression of love, caring, affection, and intimacy in adult relationships. This can cause you to confuse your need to feel comforted and safe with sex. You may actually be looking to be held and to go to sleep in someone's arms when you dive into a sexual relationship with someone too early. Even when you get involved in a committed relationship, you may not know how to express your love in other ways. You may lack the words or the affectionate gestures to let someone know your innermost thoughts and desires.

Some adult children of divorce may instead try to avoid sexual relationships with partners who seek a high level of emotional intimacy. If you're in this situation, you may feel just fine in a sexual relationship until the rest of the relationship becomes more committed. Then you may find you avoid sex as much as possible. In other words, sex is fine before marriage, but after you say "I do," you can't help but run in the opposite direction. Sex by itself is fine, but sex with intimacy and commitment can be scary beyond belief! It can be so hard for you to truly allow someone to completely love you and need you that you find it much easier to stay on the surface of the relationship. Unfortunately, you then miss out on so much more. You can always play it safe, or you can take a chance on allowing yourself to fully love someone and not separate sexuality from the rest of your intimate expressions of love. Playing it safe can be much too much of a price to pay for your parents' divorce.

Giving Too Much

Sexuality can also be compromised by the caretaker syndrome. Adult children of divorce may feel the need to please others so that they don't leave. Too often, you may sublimate yourself and your needs to those of others and focus on taking care of them at the expense of getting your needs met. This can contaminate a sexual relationship and turn it into more of a transaction, ultimately causing you to feel used or taken for granted. It can strip the intimacy and tenderness from the physical act of love.

Giving may be easier than taking because identifying your needs and desires and having them fulfilled by someone who loves you and wants to please you can be a frightening proposition as you see yourself potentially being vulnerable and even more dependent on your partner. Or perhaps worse, if you focus on your needs, you may fear your partner will reject you, claiming that you want too much. It's easy to be worried that if you get too used to being really loved, you will be much too hurt if the relationship changes and your partner leaves you. It can feel safer to work hard at caretaking and avoid thinking of yourself. Sexuality can become rather unsatisfying when you are always trying to anticipate the needs of your partner rather than allowing them to please you, thus again causing a serious impediment to authentic mutual intimacy.

Here are some helpful points to review as you embark on a sexually intimate relationship. Help yourself think clearly when your impulses may feel overwhelming.

Guidelines about Sexuality

- *Go slowly in your relationships:* It is important to be especially careful about whom you choose to have intimate physical relationships with and how you set the pace. You need a partner with whom you can have a mutual and reciprocal giving of heart and soul and not just of body. True intimacy from sexuality is nurtured with reverence and respect. It is not rushed, but something that develops over time with progressive steps towards greater sharing, closeness, and vulnerability. Your need to feel close to someone and your need to connect in a relationship quickly for fear that someone will leave you should not be the driving forces behind your decision to be physically intimate.

- *Feel safe and comfortable:* Your sexual relationship with a meaningful partner should feel very safe and comfortable. You should feel a respect and understanding of your comfort level with sexuality and its many aspects. You should not feel forced or guilty, but rather a general matching of needs and expectations in the expression of love through sexuality.

- *Communicate your feelings, likes, and dislikes:* In a healthy relationship, you need to be able to communicate freely about sexuality. You don't need to struggle to be "good enough" or be uncomfortable for fear of saying the wrong thing. The right lover wants to know what you like and dislike and respects you and your feelings.

- *Make love in countless ways:* No, we're not being provocative here. Rather, we're suggesting that you broaden your view of making love well beyond that of sexuality. Affection, loving nicknames, a thoughtful gesture, a deep shared belly laugh, a cup of tea brought without a request, or a touch on the shoulder at just the right moment are but a few ways to be making love outside of the bedroom. Children of divorce may miss seeing their parents make love in many different ways and think that sexuality is virtually the only way to express love. Seek a partner with whom you can explore the wonders of continually nurturing and loving each other in new and creative ways.

Communication

Adult children of divorce often have witnessed the worst in communication techniques and skills from their divorced parents. Conflict or silence can be two common extremes, with little or no middle ground for productive communication to exist. In your own relationships, you may struggle to figure out how to address the inevitable problems and conflicts, yet fail because you have had such poor role models. It's like trying to walk when no one has shown you or helped you develop the muscles to hold yourself up. It's all too easy to trip and flounder, trying to say what you mean, express emotion, and ask for what you need without a map and without learning the rules.

Some adult children of divorce plunge right into communications, saying whatever comes to mind without restraint and without censoring. They simply don't have a yardstick to measure and then filter their thoughts to then organize them into a coherent message. It's more like a free-flowing stream of consciousness versus a well-clarified presentation of ideas. This can lead to saying most anything that comes into your mind without regard for its impact on your partner or your relationship. It can cause you to have tumultuous relationships that are scarred by harsh words and actions. Your communications can be very raw and not always articulate what you mean to convey. After all, you've been used to hearing plenty of raw emotion expressed between your parents and may believe that it is normal to state your piece accordingly. Because the countless examples of your parents' conflict may have been very hurtful and unrestricted, your own ability to describe your feelings—especially your angry feelings—may be seriously impaired.

Close to the Vest

Another form of communication difficulties in relationships can be seen in those adult children of divorce who keep to themselves and hesitate to express any emotions for fear that they will be rejected or drive others away. If this pertains to you, you're likely to be quiet, shy, and cautious. You would rather say nothing than risk saying the wrong thing and having your partner angry or upset with you. You may deny or ignore your own needs and feelings, suppressing any desire to articulate them. You may avoid interpersonal conflict at all costs. As a child, you may never have learned to communicate assertively, to put forth your own wishes in a succinct, respectful, and well-thought-out manner. If these patterns routinely persist, you may find yourself unaware of what you think and feel, which can create a level of emotional dependency and strain in your intimate relationships. Your emotional anonymity, desire to please, and worry about saying the right thing can actually drive others away. Partners can only read your mind for so long as they try to guess what you feel and need. They can get tired of this and decide that they need to find someone who can offer authentic feelings and interact in a more equal manner. Others may take advantage of this tendency by forming an autocratic relationship where their feelings and desires take precedence over yours. When you figure this out and start to speak your mind, you may find that the relationship comes to an end because it may not have matured enough to be ready to tolerate the change in roles and dynamics. If you picked someone who enjoys running the show, you may have no choice but to revert back or to leave. Isn't that just what you wanted to avoid in the first place? Practicing clear communication is the best way to invest in your relationships.

But, practicing clear communication is not always so easy. It requires a lot of self-awareness and a repeated focus on some basic elements. We offer you the following guidelines to help you consider some general approaches to healthy communication and to help you communicate clearly in your romantic relationships. Use these guidelines to prevent impulsive communication or the silence that can occur when the thought of communicating makes you fearful.

Guidelines about Communication

- *Keep the noise to a minimum:* It's good to express yourself, but you should be careful to make sure that you express exactly what you want and not all the other superfluous noise that is so easily attached. Assertive communication is thoughtful, careful, succinct, and very respectful. It focuses on developing a clear presentation of the problem while offering a workable solution.

- *Seek models and teachers of healthy communication:* It's likely that your parents were not the best role models for effective communication and conflict resolution. You need to have new teachers who can help you learn to reflect and communicate assertively and appropriately. These teachers can be your partner or others who can give you feedback, listen, and demonstrate healthy strategies for productive communication.

- *Avoid avoidance:* Avoidance, denial, or passivity will most certainly only leave you in a more precarious position in your relationships. Changing this pattern can be new and, at times, scary for you, especially if you survived your parents' divorce by trying to stay out of the way and keep a low profile. With the help and love of your partner (and maybe even a therapist at some point), you can learn to effectively and appropriately state your piece and voice your emotional needs. Communication cannot hurt more than the confusion, resentment, and empty voids of silence present in relationships where the partners are afraid to take the risk of being open and honest with each other.

Developing Commitment— Believing in Yourself

Given all that has been discussed in the above sections of this chapter, you may feel that taking back your love life will be a daunting task. You may feel overwhelmed and disheartened and see the journey ahead as a winding, uphill climb without guardrails. You may be scared, uncertain, and very unsure of yourself in this domain. But take heart, because if you dare, you can experience the best that life has to offer—a truly loving relationship. Yes, it can be possible for you, too, even if you still feel as if you're an injured adult child of divorce. You may not think so, but someone's love may be there for you completely and forever.

You're probably saying, "How can I be in a permanent and loving relationship when I've been crippled by my parents' divorce and maybe even more so by their continued conflict and inability to parent me and my siblings? They didn't show me anything about how to love someone completely and without reserve, so I don't know the first thing about how to form and foster a real loving relationship today and well on into the future." Here again, you're allowing your old thought patterns to control you. Even if you were a child in a highly conflictual family, you have learned about love during your life.

Journal Exercise 9.3

Think about what you experienced in your family about loving relationships. Write down your thoughts in your journal.

- Describe what made you feel bad.

- What would you have liked to have experienced?

- How should the loving relationship have been demonstrated?

- What should a committed relationship really be like?

Answering the questions in this exercise can help you find clues to what you actually have learned about relationships. You're not as ignorant and helpless as you might first believe. Even young children can have an idea about how relationships should work. They can be most articulate about what is wrong, not fair, or unkind. You likely had these concepts as a child. They are just covered over by the pain and subsequent learning that incorrectly told you that you can't trust what your inner self knows to be true.

Below are some basic guidelines for developing a committed relationship with someone whom you love and who says that they love you, too. One wise adult child of divorce put it so aptly when she said, "I don't know how to love. My parents were divorced." So let's now get started on the right track. The following guidelines will head you in the right direction.

Guidelines about Commitment

- *Let go of your old fears:* Press that "stop" button on the tape that is playing your old negative and depressing songs. Sure, it's easier to repeat those old words. You already know them well and their familiarity is *so* comfortable. But that comfort level will only prevent you from daring to believe and from daring to try. You need to recognize that fear is paralyzing and stagnating your love life. So take the opportunity on a new world. Allow someone the opportunity to help you grow, to be vulnerable, and to love completely. Your fear is understandable, but you don't have to let it give you relationship paralysis. You can experience fear and still decide to take the chance to also experience the excitement, warmth, and eventual safety of an intimate and loving relationship. If you cannot do this for yourself or with the help of a significant other, you may need to find a competent therapist to help you sort out the issues and their origins and to support you in taking the steps that can change your life and allow the seeds of genuine love, affection, and interdependence to flourish.

- *Take a chance:* In order to have love in your life, you must be willing to take a chance! You just might be able to achieve something that your parents could not maintain or never had in the first place. But you cannot do this without risking the possibility that you may be hurt, and you surely will feel vulnerable. You may feel like you're standing on the edge of a large ravine with the chance at love on the other side. You are afraid of heights, but you know that crossing the rickety bridge in front of you may save your life. Someone you believe you love and can trust is saying, "Hold my hand, and we'll cross together." The risks here are great, but the rewards can be more than worth it.

- *See the positives in your significant other:* It's all too easy to focus on the negative aspects of anyone in your life. Finding fault is simple, but looking at the positive is a lot better way to build a relationship, even if it feels scary. If you focus on what is good, then you just may decide to hold onto the relationship and not dismiss it too soon.

- *No relationship is perfect:* You may have grown up in a household where conflict abounded and the emphasis was on what was wrong and not on what was right. It's even possible that there was a lot wrong, and so you're not even sure of a good thing when you see it. Try to see what might be working for you and not what might go wrong. Look for reasons to say yes. Saying yes may scare you, but just think about the positive consequences.

- *Take your time, but not too much:* It's certainly important to be thoughtful and to apply criteria to your choices in relationship partners. Nonetheless, you can also wait too long to choose. If you tend to hesitate excessively and evaluate every little nuance of a person and your relationship, you may just miss out on the love of your life. Most potential life partners will not wait around forever. Nor will they tolerate endless tests of their worth and love. At some point you will both feel the need to fish or cut bait and be either in or out of the relationship. Those of you who are more commitment-shy will find any excuse to evaluate and wait. You set up countless hoops to jump through with no endpoint in sight. Applying rational thinking is important, but analyzing every detail over and over from every angle is not. Don't "shrink" the relationship to death! At some point you need to follow your heart.

- *Pay attention to the "us"*: A relationship is an "us" thing and not an "I" thing. In order to be successful in a relationship, you need to start to think differently. Growing up in a single-parent family changes your perspective as you learn to focus on yourself without any opportunity to see a working marriage where partners are focused on the goal of nurturing and pleasing each other. When there is mutual nurturance of each other, both people can feel cared for. Each person does not have to selfishly worry about first taking care of their own needs because each of you is too busy doing that for each other. A committed relationship can thrive beautifully when both partners give to the "us" (the couple) and stop trying to make sure that their own unique individual needs are met. The "us" is like an emotional savings account that, when routinely contributed to, can allow the relationship to be strong and healthy for a long time. Too many relationships fall apart because the partners are too busy worrying about taking care of themselves as individuals instead of feeding the joint entity formed by the two of them together.

- *Lock the back door labeled "D"*: Love relationships need to not have open back doors and simple escape clauses. If either partner feels that there is an easy exit, they may not work at the relationship with all the time, energy, and commitment that are available and needed for a relationship of such importance. The back door can seem pretty appealing and a whole lot easier than trying to work at something during the hard times. The "D" (Divorce) door often feels like an option for adult children of divorce more than it does for adults from intact families. You are all too familiar with the possibility and know all the statistics about the probability. Even though you may know the painful conflict of divorce very well, you may see leaving as an option that is easier than staying to trudge through the tough periods. It's important that you and your partner feel that a committed relationship is a closed circuit so that you give it your all and don't look for the way out as soon as the going gets a bit rough.

Recognize the Love in Your Heart

Relationships are the very seeds of your soul. Love relationships are the very sustenance for your heart. Do not be afraid to love and to be loved. Your history may have been riddled with pain and fear, but the way to move forward is to believe in the possibility that you can love and be loved better than your parents. When you let the past and your childhood experiences and emotions dictate the present, you relinquish control over your own life and give it back to your parents. You can change this if you choose to do so and want something more for yourself. Healthy relationships can help rebuild trust, hope, and dreams. Decide to live your most important relationships on your own terms and not those of your parents. Their divorce or life alone does *not* have to be your destiny. The choice is yours. Choose wisely and choose to love with all your heart and soul.

Chapter 10

Having Children: Rekindling Your Parenting Desires

As an adult child of divorce, you might find that you are torn about whether or not to have children. You experienced so much pain after the end of your parents' marriage and might question why anyone in their right mind would want to bring a child into the world only to possibly face the same fate. Perhaps you ask yourself, "Why would I take the risk of loving a child, only to have them spend 50 percent of their time away from me if I get divorced?" You might think of the anger you had toward one or both parents and be fearful of the possibility that your children could come to be as angry or hateful toward you. That might seem like more than you think you could endure.

On the other hand, children can be far from just screaming, demanding, and distant. They can bring you a special joy as you participate in life with them. You help them grow, learn about life, face challenges, and experience the pleasure of their successes. The unique bond between parent and child in a healthy relationship is like nothing else. It's different than adult relationships or any other relationship you may have had, and it certainly can be different than your relationships with your parents. While you struggle about learning to parent, your child trusts you from the start. While you wonder about your own abilities and go through your own adult challenges, your young child learns from you. From the complex skills associated with physical movement and language to the demands of learning to get along with others, your children will take their cues from you. They are consummate observers, even when they don't look like they care or are paying attention. Older children will criticize you and find every one of your flaws (even ones you don't think you have), yet the connection between parent and child will still remain a unique bond. This connection is so strong that, as we said earlier, alienated children often feel tremendous anger rather than the indifference you might expect if one disrespected an individual to whom there was no emotional connection. That is, it's the strong underlying emotional connection that causes the strong emotion of anger.

So, do you play it safe or take the risk of experiencing an opportunity for an amazing connection and the chance to help raise another human being? If you opt for parenting, you should make sure that you have some fundamentals in place to help you along the way. Keep in mind that "along the way" doesn't just refer to the time from conception until your child's eighteenth birthday. Rather, it applies to your child's life span. Or at least your life span in the context of your child's life. Your relationship with your child may easily span fifty to sixty years. In fact, most of the relationship will occur after (not during) your child's youth. Yet, what occurs in your child's youth will have a profound impact on the later parent/child relationship.

Some of the fundamentals we discuss in this chapter are related to

- Creating your own parental support system

- Building a coparenting relationship with your partner

- Learning to show parental love

- Building healthy parent/child relationships

- Fostering healthy adult relationships with your children

We believe these fundamentals will go a long way toward helping you traverse the journey of parenthood. Yet, as an adult child of divorce, you may not have had experience observing some of these fundamentals exhibited by your parents. You might not even believe the fundamentals are possible because of your experiences and the negative beliefs that they have caused.

For example, if you still believe that in some way you were responsible for your parents' divorce or failure to reconcile, you might be saying to yourself, "I ruined my parents' relationship. If I spoiled their relationship and their lives, I know I will spoil the life of any child I try to raise." It is crucially important to challenge this belief and to repeatedly remind yourself that you were *not*, in any way, responsible for your parents' divorce and for what happened to their lives and relationships. Children don't cause divorces—parents do. Children can't ruin marriages. You were not "the spoiler." You simply didn't have the power. You also didn't have the power to spoil your relationship with one or both of your parents. Your relationships with your children can be quite different from your relationships with your parents.

Confronting your irrational negative beliefs and building on the elements described in this chapter can help you travel the road of parenthood, facing the unknowns of the journey with more ease and success.

Creating Your Own Parental Support System

Talk to any parent and they will tell you that the joys of parenting are at times counterbalanced by its demands and stresses. It's easy for you to become depleted. Whether single or with a partner, working out of the house or not, gay or straight, in a miserable adult relationship or a healthy one, raising one child or many, or raising a teenager who is emerging as an independent adult, you are constantly giving support in an emotional and at times physical manner. This puts you in a position of delaying your own needs as you take care of your child, family, work, and friends. "Later" may become a familiar mantra when it comes to your own needs. Others may even accuse you of being selfish for thinking about taking care of yourself. How can you work out, go on vacation, or be with friends when you have so many responsibilities?

Add to this the questions and uncertainty associated with raising a child. You may ask yourself, "Am I doing this right?" or "How should I handle _____ ?" For new parents, the simplest decisions can take on incredible importance as you wrestle with the indecision around which brand of diapers to buy and the confusion about why the baby is sleeping for so long as you contemplate waking them up.

You have stress, emotional depletion, physical exhaustion, confusion, and uncertainty all operating in concert to lead you into the abyss and to cause you to lose your perspective. If you feel burned out in your parental role, you might find yourself pondering in a guilt-inducing manner, "Now what's so good about being a parent?"

It might surprise you to find out that you're not alone. Most parents (whether adult children of divorce or not) struggle with the same or very similar issues. Some feel alone and isolated with little validation for what they feel and little opportunity to benefit from the friendship, camaraderie, and advice of other parents. But eventually, most parents find that the support of other caring individuals can be crucial to helping them get through the difficult moments of parenting.

There is no magic to creating your own support system. There may be a little luck involved if you happen to have one already in place or just fall in with a supportive group of other parents. However, most of the time finding a support group requires a bit more work as well as patience, persistence, and a willingness to be flexible and accepting. At times, you may need to change groups or individuals with whom you relate for support. At other times, you may need to recognize that your support system has flaws and cannot address all your needs in a sufficient (let alone perfect) fashion. Nevertheless, a support system can be a major building block or foundation for parents as they raise their children.

We have listed below different types of relationships where you may be able to find support as a parent. Most of these are informal networks of two or more people. Some are more formal support groups as well.

- Lunch groups at work

- Other parents at community activities

- Parents at your child's play groups

- Your own friends and possibly family

- Older adults who have already "been there"

- Immediate and other extended family members

- Parents Without Partners

- Parents Anonymous

- Therapist-run support groups

- Parents who you see regularly at your extracurricular activities

- Your primary partner

The trick is being open to finding the right person(s) for you. You need to feel that you can safely ask questions or talk about your feelings with the people from whom you seek support. This support can help fill the voids caused by the inevitable depletions you face as a parent and by the self-doubts that were caused by your own experiences during and after your parents' divorce.

Coparenting with Your Partner

You and your partner begin a committed relationship to one another, two against the world. You are together, nurturing, and reinforcing each other. The "us" is a twosome. It's easy to focus on each other, as there are few other distractions. It's almost as if there is a never-ending dance going on where you and your partner are always taking care of one or the other of you. This can build a unifying bond between you. Unfortunately, many couples are unprepared for the impact of parenthood on their relationship and the need for their relationship to shift in a special way to accommodate the arrival of a child.

The presence of a child immediately offsets the balance in the relationship of two partners who mutually support and care for each other as each partner's needs become secondary to that of the child. In fact, in many families both partners can feel ignored and trivialized as they almost exclusively focus on taking care of the child. New parents may rarely get a baby-sitter. They may go from an almost exclusive focus to almost never focusing on one another. Imagine that 90 percent of the emotional energy in the couple was split between the partners before the child was born (45/45). After the child is present, let's assume the same level of emotional energy (90 percent) goes to the child. Only 5 percent of the total emotional energy is then left for each parent. Even parents who are far from self-centered can feel left out and be saying, "Hey, what about me? When is it my turn?" They can resent each other and even, at some level, resent the child and then feel guilty about these resentments.

This dynamic can remind you of how your parents may have seemed to feel. You can even find yourself saying, "I know just how Mom/Dad felt—left out and unimportant. I feel as unsupported and trivial as they felt. What's my own marriage coming to? How did I get here? I know I'm on the same track as my parents were before their divorce."

All of this pushes against you, your partner, and your relationship, while at the same time you have a child who needs your combined focus and the best that you both have to give as parents. Building a coparenting relationship can help, but it requires a great deal of consistency in focus or mission between the two of you.

Below are some guidelines for structuring a healthy coparenting relationship. By all means, you should feel free to discuss these with your partner and try to come to some common understandings.

Guidelines for Healthy Coparenting

- *Separate out your relationship as coparents from your relationship as a couple:* Recognize that from the vantage point of your child(ren), you are parents more than you are a couple. Even if the "couple" is no longer present, the love your child has for you as parents should always remain. Additionally, if you recognize that you are really in two roles (parents and couple), you can concentrate your attention at different times on each of those different roles and the needs you have within each role.

- *Agree that you will always be parents together for your child:* Your role as parents needs to come before whatever happens in your role as partners. Even on a day-to-day basis, your commitment to your child needs to be the dominant factor, causing you to respond appropriately to your child and not to your issues as adults.

- *Agree on common values:* Many parents get sidetracked into arguing about those aspects of parenting upon which they do not agree and consequently lose sight of the very many values that they share. It is, in some ways, more important to be acutely aware of those areas of parenting that you and your partner have in common. These can help guide you in your routine actions and also in the difficult decisions that are ahead.

- *Recognize that parenting is one of the most emotional tasks you will face:* There is perhaps no other task in life that is as subjective as parenting. Your childhood experiences, personal values, emotional or ego investment in being a parent, and your love for your child can easily cause both of you to view parenting with less objectivity than you have in other areas of your life. Give each other room to be more sensitive and perhaps a bit less rational at times.

- *Communicate frequently:* So many parents don't communicate frequently or effectively, causing confusion and resentment. It can be helpful to develop routines where you regularly communicate with one another about your child(ren). Some parents find that they have little rituals, such as having coffee together in the morning, washing the dishes at night together, or sitting on the couch after dinner, when they talk about the events of the day and the needs of the children. This builds a structure so that you are prepared for your communication with one another and not trying to communicate at awkward times (and surprised when the communication is not effective).

- *Share the burdens and the pleasures:* Clearly delegate who will do what, but don't keep a tally sheet. Parenting is not about fairness. It's about loving and doing what needs to be done. It is your job together to see to it that your child's needs are addressed and that your child feels the love that both of you have for them. On the other hand, make sure you share the pleasures of parenthood as well. While there are going to be times when you feel you have an unequal share of the burdens, you should always be looking for ways to bring the other parent into the pleasures and good times of parenting. Instead of saying, "I'm sorry you missed Rebecca's dance recital today. She was great!" you could say, "After dinner I want us to sit down with Rebecca. Her dance recital was today, and I taped it so you could have the chance to see Rebecca the way I did today." That way the other parent and Rebecca share the joys of this special event.

- *Don't forget to take care of the couple:* Taking care of the couple is very important. While children can grow up just fine in single-parent families and in families where marriages are dysfunctional, they also clearly benefit from the closeness and warmth they sense between their parents. Pay attention to each other, and you will be giving your children important gifts—parents who feel good about their relationship and are role models for the child's later adult relationships.

The better the two of you work as a team, the more your children will benefit. Your adult relationship as partners should enhance your ability to be in sync as parents providing a loving atmosphere for your child to grow and thrive.

Committing to the Children

Parents often tell us how committed they are to their children. They say, "I'd lay down my life for my child," or "If a truck was coming, I'd throw myself in front of it to save my child." These are wonderful expressions of love, however coparenting is not so simple as a single dramatic gesture. It requires quality communication, mutual respect, and effective decision making and problem solving focused on addressing the needs of the children.

Think back to your own childhood for a moment. Did you feel that your parents were committed to you, no matter what? Or, did you feel that you were, in a sense, pushed to the side as they argued, divorced, and competed for the "parent of the year" award? Did their commitment to you cause them to rise above their own anxieties, pain, and depression, or were you left to take care of yourself and them, too? It may be hard for you to believe that one can truly be committed as a parent.

Even the commitments voiced above are one-time actions. It is relatively easy to walk through fire once to save your child. However, on a day-to-day basis, working together with your child's other parent requires a different sense of persistent commitment. Whether you are married to your child's other parent or not, coparenting requires you to be ever cognizant of your joint roles and the need to work together. The commitment to your children is necessary not only on good days, but on days when you are tired, got yelled at by your boss, face financial stresses, are angry at your partner, and feel isolated, insecure, and alone. The commitment to work together for the children requires the two of you to put these other issues aside for the moment and figure out how best to address your child's needs at a given time.

This is best accomplished by looking at the situation and yourselves through your child's eyes. This doesn't mean that you think as a nine-year-old. Rather, it means that you use your child's viewpoint to help guide your actions, recognizing that your adult behavior will be interpreted through your child's less mature system of perceptions. For example, let's assume that soccer practice is every Saturday morning. Your partner works long hours, and even before the child was born, loved to sleep late on Saturdays. It is a little gift that they give themselves. Perhaps you played soccer as a child and still love the game. It would be relatively easy for you to take over soccer and to fall into the trap of letting your partner sleep late and rarely attend a Saturday game. Your partner may be involved in many other areas of your child's life, and you both may feel this is a reasonable compromise or distribution of responsibility. However, things are not so simple, because your child may feel that this parent has little interest in them and something as important to them as soccer. Your child may not be able to have an adult view (even if you explain the situation). In cases such as these, your coparenting commitment may inspire the two of you as parents to have a talk about the decision to sleep in during soccer season. It might be much better to show the child that they are important enough to wake up for on Saturday mornings. It's your commitment to your child that causes you to sit down, talk to one another, and risk not taking the easy way out by avoiding the discussion.

Now imagine that the situation is more complex. Perhaps there are strong and opposing feelings involved on both your parts. Does that change the need to work together? Does it change your commitment to work together for your child? Or, does it mean that now is the time to actually demonstrate that commitment? That is, the commitment needs to be obvious during the difficult times, not just the easy times. For example, divorced parents often tell us with pride that they both go to school plays. Yet, when we ask them where they sit, we find that they sit on different sides of the auditorium. So, when the play is over, their child comes down from the stage and has to first locate both parents and then deal with the dreaded decision of who to see first. Are these parents truly committed to their child at that time, or are they still thinking about their own needs (the need to see the child's play but not sit anywhere near the other parent). If they were working optimally as coparents, wouldn't they be sitting close enough to one another so that when the lights came on after the play, they could be standing together in the same aisle? That way, the child can run up to them without the pressure of a loyalty conflict. The commitment needs to be apparent even at school plays, around the little things, and when it is *not* easy, comfortable, or an emergency.

As parents, you can highlight this commitment by discussing different situations within the simple frameworks of

- What would be best for our child?

- What do we want our child to learn or experience from this situation?

- How will our child interpret our actions and words?

By discussing the many parenting decisions ahead using these questions, you can make sure that you are demonstrating your commitment by working together in the best interests of your child and not merely from your own viewpoints.

Showing Love

Do some of these quotes sound familiar?

- "Of course I love you."

- "Don't you realize the reason I work so hard is because I love you and I'm trying to provide for you as best I can?"

- "The reason I'm saying no is because I love you."

- "If I give in, you will think I'm weak."

- "I can't be affectionate with my kids because my parents weren't affectionate with me. We just don't show love that way, but my kids know I love them."

Do you think children just "know" they are loved? Or are the statements above simply rationalizations by parents to avoid taking the emotional risk to communicate love in a meaningful way, in a way that is clearly understood by children?

Below or in your journal, list the things that you do for your child (or would do when you have children) because you love them.

Journal Exercise 10.1

1.

2.

3.

4.

5.

How many of the above behaviors do you think a child would instinctively recognize as a sign of your love? How similar or different are your behaviors from those of your parents?

Below is a list of some behaviors that parents think they do because they love their child, but may be hard for the child to recognize as "loving." Are some of these behaviors on your list?

- Saving money for college tuition

- Disciplining your child

- Teasing your child in a loving way

- Working hard

- Doing household chores that benefit the child

- Enrolling the child in special or expensive extracurricular activities

- Showing your child how their life is better than yours was at their age

- Teaching your child values

- Making sure your child cleans their room and does homework on a regular basis

- Taking your child on a vacation

Imagine the frustration felt by some parents as they do these things and their children don't appreciate or recognize the love that is behind the parent's actions. We are not saying these behaviors are wrong. To the contrary, these are important behaviors in which parents should engage. But you might bear in mind that it is unlikely that children will actually appreciate these behaviors (especially before adulthood).

From an opposite perspective, use the worksheet below or your journal to list up to five things your parents did when you were a child that showed you back then that they loved you.

Journal Exercise 10.2

1.

2.

3.

4.

5.

If your parents had a high-conflict divorce, you may find that the above exercise was quite difficult.

Now list five behaviors that you would have liked for them to have done.

Journal Exercise 10.3

1.

2.

3.

4.

5.

Would it be difficult to go ahead and implement behaviors that show your love on a regular basis? In all likelihood, they are not expensive and do not take much time. You can use your commitment to your child as a motivation for engaging in behaviors that more clearly show your love to your child. Does your child need to figure it out, or can you show them in such a way that they can easily recognize your love? Of course you can! There are probably no adequate justifications that could rationalize not showing your love in a clear, obvious way.

Some parents will actually support each other by prompting the other to show love in ways that each is not normally inclined. For example, if I am not very "touchy-feely" and you are, it could be really helpful for you to suggest to me that our child needs a hug after a major disappointment. I might be tempted to simply say to our child, "That's too bad. Maybe you'll do better next time." However, that might not be nearly enough. Your suggestion of, "I think [the child] could really use a hug right now," could go a long way.

Here is a short list of behaviors that might likely be perceived by children as a sign of your love.

- Giving an unexpected hug "just because"

- Saying, "I love you"

- Being involved in extracurricular activities

- Telling your child, "I'm proud of you"

- Saying, "I'm sorry"

- Saying, "You were right"

- Paying attention to what your child is saying and not asking them questions that they've just answered

- Having one-on-one time with your child (without your partner or your child's siblings)

- Having dinner with your child on a regular basis

- Letting the answering machine pick up when you are with your child

- Kissing your child good night *every* night

Now list five more behaviors that you don't presently do, but could do that would be obvious signs (even to a young child) of your love.

Journal Exercise 10.4

1.

2.

3.

4.

5.

Of course you can show your love. Your busy life, painful history, and other distractions don't have to keep you from giving your child your love in ways they can see and feel to their core.

Building Healthy Parent/Child Relationships

From the moment of creation, a process of growth, development, individuation, and independence begins. Your child's life begins as merely two cells. These cells grow and are totally dependent upon the mother while in utero. At birth, a major step toward independence begins as the baby begins to breathe on its own and make its needs known. Yet, it's still very dependent on others (primarily its parents) for food, hygiene, shelter, and long-term survival. As your child grows, they begin to be able to take care of their basic needs and wants. Your child learns to move through space, reach for and pick up things they want, and feed themselves. Your child then learns to manipulate their environment (and you, too) and develops opinions. They begin to learn to differentiate self from others and learn the difficult lesson that they aren't the center of the universe. Over time and through formal and informal learning, your child continues to grow, learning to read, get along with others, and address more complex social and intellectual needs. Eventually your child moves out of your home and becomes even more independent as they prepare for adult life and for the cycle to begin anew when your child becomes a parent.

While there are many forms the journey to adulthood can take, it's a trip that most children and their parents will go through together. The question then becomes one of *how* the journey will take place and what the parent/child relationship will be like throughout the life span.

In thinking about this section of the chapter, we feared we could fall into the trap of trying to teach you how to be the "perfect" parent. However, we quickly realized that while many authors have seemingly tried to impart this wisdom, there isn't yet one authoritative source for raising children. We decided that neither other authors nor we could tell anyone exactly how to be parents. There is no particular formula that, when followed, will reliably lead to success. Rather, we decided to use this part of the chapter to list some guidelines for healthy parent/child relationships. You will have to decide how and when to use these guidelines and which ones will be most useful to you in your own parenting. These guidelines are not new or unique. We have acquired them from years of clinical and personal experience and the writings of many authors. Our hope here is that you can use them as helpful frameworks to support the parenting skills you already have. As you read through them, see which ones were followed by your parents. You might want to pay special attention to areas that you think were *not* well emphasized by your parents, or were especially not attended to as a function of their divorce.

Build Trust

Perhaps one of the central features of a healthy parent/child relationship is that of trust. You build trust by showing your child that you reliably take care of and love them. This comes from your child repeatedly and positively experiencing a consistency between what you say and what you do over time. The word "positively" is quite important to the concept of parent/child trust. Trust between a parent and a child is clearly enhanced when parents can be perceived as nurturing and caring, dedicated to taking care of their children and not just their own needs.

Show Unconditional Love

Imagine feeling that two people love you just as you are, simply for being *you*. If you felt this as a child, you have a lot to be thankful for. Unfortunately, many children do not feel unconditional love—even when it's there. We suspect that this is so because parents often have difficulty demonstrating unconditional love. As parents, we are often quick to try to teach our child a lesson during their difficult times. So we say things such as, "That's okay. I know you feel bad about [the situation]. Maybe next time if you [do this] it will work out better." What does the child hear most? In all likelihood the child hears the parent saying, "I'm sorry you didn't do better in [the situation]. If you would have just done this, both you and I would have been more pleased." If you want to show unconditional love, you might consider not trying to solve the problem right away. You might instead just try to be supportive so as not to have the message of support confused with what the child could have done differently. You might have simply put your arm around the child and said, "I'm so sorry that you're disappointed. You know, to me it doesn't change a thing. I love you, and I'm here for you if I can help." You will not be able to solve all of your child's problems. Routinely focusing on solutions can take away from the basic premise of your love for the child. Is it more important for your child to have the solution (which, by the way, they may already know) or to know unequivocally that they have your support? We think the important message is knowing that they have your support, especially when they made a mistake in the first place.

Set Limits

Some parents (and professionals) seem to confuse unconditional love with unconditional parenting. As a parent, you have the responsibility to teach your child restraint and impulse control. Civilized society is based on a combination of freedom and restraint. Children need to learn appropriate limits so they can avoid danger, be socially appropriate, and learn to not simply respond to the impulse of the moment, but rather make decisions that are in their best interests. The parent who scolds a five-year-old for running out into the street or hitting their sibling is setting a limit out of love for the child. However, it's highly unlikely that the child will perceive this parent's behavior as loving. Setting limits also may be highly conditional and even stated as such. For example, you might say, "If you want to stay up later tonight, you have to eat your dinner." It is the privilege of staying up later (not the parental love) that is conditional in this example.

Keep Healthy Boundaries

This is often quite difficult for parents, especially during times of stress. Your divorcing parents may have had particular problems with boundaries. Parents can be too distant or too close. They can be inattentive or smother their child with attention. They can never share their feelings with their child or let their child into their own fears and sadness and the other dark corners of their soul. Parents can generally avoid affection or be so affectionate that their children begin to feel uncomfortable or responsible for nurturing the parent. It's difficult to know exactly where to draw the line. Furthermore, as your child grows, the line keeps changing. For example, taking a bath with your baby may be okay. However, at a certain point you stop joining your child in the tub. At another point, you don't even stay in the bathroom when they bathe. Instead, you knock on the door before you enter and say, "Are you decent? Can I come in?" At some level, this may seem a bit ridiculous. After all, you've raised this child since infancy. But it's essential that you vary and maintain new boundaries as the child grows.

Respect Your Child

Many parents expect that their children will be smaller but better versions of who they are themselves. Yet children are by their very nature quite different from their parents. In fact, as a child moves into adolescence they may want to accentuate this difference as they become more independent. You may find that your child doesn't share your likes and dislikes. You love golf, they hate it. You were a good, dedicated student, they are not. You do not have a very spiritual foundation, and they are becoming deeply religious. You are outgoing and they are shy. You are an accountant, and your child wants to be a physical-fitness teacher. Who's right? Hopefully, your choices are right for you. More importantly, your child needs to feel that you respect the process of their making choices for themselves and that you respect them even for being different from you.

Distinguish Your Child's Worth from Accomplishments

Almost everything we see and hear tells us that our individual worth is based on our accomplishments. Even as you read this last sentence you might be saying to yourself, "Well, if not that, what then?" Yet, if you think about a newborn child's worth (especially if it was *your* newborn child) you might readily say that the child has worth even though it has accomplished little and won't be able to accomplish much for some time. In other words, you might recognize that the child has inherent worth. Unfortunately, this principle of inherent worth quickly gets lost in the social dynamics of our culture. As you and your children observe your environment, you see people who excel all around you. Your peers spell better, catch a ball better, get better grades, get into better colleges, have better jobs, make more money, have more successful family lives, have more prestige, and get more respect from others (including their parents and children). And you know, you're right! Wherever you look you can find someone who does or has something more (or less) than you. But this doesn't change the inherent worth that has been present since (or even before) birth. *Worth* does not change. What we *do* changes and can be more or less successful. We may fail at a task, but that does not make us "failures." Children need us to counterbalance the social messages that confuse this concept and damage their self-esteem.

Let Them Be Independent Risk Takers

One of the basic parental instincts that we have is to keep our children safe from harm, especially foreseeable harm. We certainly don't want our children to suffer the pain of making the same mistakes we've made. As parents, we can often easily see all the "yes, buts" or the things that can possibly go wrong. We program this into ourselves from the day we bring the baby home from the hospital and start to think about food, blankets, open windows, the width between the crib bars, and so on. Yet, if we are overprotective, our children learn to be overly dependent on us and learn to avoid reasonable risks. They may even view themselves as weak and incapable of trying new things. The trick here is to help children learn how to make reasonable decisions. However, again the bar keeps moving, because what is not reasonable at one age can be very appropriate at another. We need to allow children to grow by allowing them to try new things and even at times by literally and figuratively allowing them to bruise a knee or two as they learn how to ride the bicycle of life.

Choose Your Battles

There is a tension that is very normal to the parenting process. As children learn to think for themselves, they will normally challenge much of what is so basic and fundamental to you. You may hear, "I want three cookies, not two" or, "It's my room, I can keep it the way I want." Or, you may hear, "It's my body, if I want to get it pierced, I will." If you fight all or none of the battles, you will not be teaching your child about what is important to you. They will learn that everything is essentially the same, either a "10" or a "0" on a ten-point scale. By picking your battles carefully, your children can learn that they have the freedom to make some mistakes for themselves, and that when you are really invested in the conflict, it may be for a very good reason. This may be a very different concept for you if your parents divorced with significant conflict and you experienced everything as a battle or a "10."

Remember, there are no clear recipes for success as a parent. However, keeping the uniqueness of your children in mind as you and your partner raise them can go a long way toward allowing your children to benefit from seeing and experiencing the love you have for them. But, it doesn't stop there.

Healthy Adult Relationships with Your Children

While the process of growth, independence, and individuation progresses through the life span, there is an amazing feature that is perhaps unique to humans and only a few other species. The parent/child connection can remain intact even after the child is completely grown and self-sufficient. Even in severely dysfunctional families, the connections of the parents to the children can still be in place. Perhaps one of the greatest but least acknowledged joys of parenthood can come from spending twenty to thirty years of adult life in a relationship with your children and their respective nuclear families. Here the bond of family can bring a special closeness and joy, while at the same time giving you the support, friendship and mutual respect associated with a caring and loving adult parent/child relationship.

Here again we find that the same principles about trust, boundaries, communication, and the others stated above become quite relevant, and perhaps even more so. Adult children may be less tolerant than young children. They are not forced to be in a relationship with us and have many competing influences that can distract them or pull them away from us. As parents, we need to recognize the importance of working on the relationship and being a pleasant source of support for our children. We cannot assume that it's their turn to tolerate and take care of us. Rather, we need to assume that our children are still looking for our support, love, and respect. They still want to feel that we care.

Below are some basic guidelines for having a relationship with your adult children. As with the guidelines in the section above, they are not all-inclusive and are meant to help you recognize that you have choices and priorities in dealing with your adult children.

Freely Offer Support

Kids of all ages need to be able to count on their parents. Most of the time, they may simply need to know that you're there if they need you. This knowledge may help them feel secure enough to take the chance to solve problems on their own and may actually cause them to say to you, "That's okay, I can take care of it myself." Feel free to often say, "You know, I'm here for you. Just let me know if I can help."

Offer Suggestions Sparingly

Adult children often dislike being told what to do or that you know best about what is good for them. Rather than immediately offering suggestions, you may find it more useful to say something such as, "Let me know if you need any ideas about that" or, "Do you want some suggestions about that?"

Have Fun with Your Children

Yes, that's right—have fun. You don't have to be a stuffy parent to your adult children. They will probably enjoy watching you smile and enjoy yourself. You will also be showing them that they can have fun with their children. Grandparents don't have to sit on the couch or stand on the sidelines. They can get down on the floor, get on the sled, or kick the soccer ball, too.

Give Your Children Space

Just as you need to maintain appropriate boundaries with your parents, so do your children need their boundaries respected by you. You certainly can be an important part of their life but can also respect their need to sometimes go their own way on different days and make decisions that you might not directly approve of. There are times they will choose to be with other extended family members or friends, rather than with you. They may make different lifestyle decisions than you would like for them. They nevertheless need to be free to build their own life, yet know that the connection with you (not your direct influence over them) is strong.

Don't Make Money an Issue

Your adult children don't always need to be taught lessons about money. Sometimes your generosity can go a long way, making it easy for them to spend time with you, enjoy themselves, or offer their children a special experience. Other times, allowing your children to pay for something can give them a sense that you respect where they are in life and their own ability to be in an adult role with you. Don't allow financial issues to become distancers between you and your children.

Maintain a Confidence

If you want your children to trust you and be open with you, then you need to make sure that you act in a manner that fosters those feelings. You need to be extremely careful about revealing confidences without your child's permission. Even an accidental "slip" can cause a serious erosion of trust. Be careful to make sure you ask whether a sensitive issue should be kept in confidence. Don't assume that because they haven't asked you to keep the confidence that they don't expect you to do so. Also, be very careful about assuming that because they've told you something of a sensitive nature, that they've also told their partner or someone else. There are times when you may be the only one to whom they disclose something or from whom they seek advice.

Don't "Yes, But"

That's right, you can ask your children for help and advice. It doesn't make you lose face. In fact, it can help your child see that you are human and need them. It can also give them a sense that you recognize their competencies and value their strengths and abilities. Be careful, however, to make sure you avoid seeking their advice and then telling them that their ideas are not useful. Saying, "That's a good idea, but . . ." is a good way to inadvertently give your child the message that you don't really value their opinion. Sometimes it can be better to simply listen to their suggestion and tell them you will think it over without committing to follow it.

Tell Them You Love Them

Most children are never too old to hear their parents tell them that they love them and are proud of them. You may think, "Of course my child knows that." Yet, many children just don't realize that their parents are proud of them. They may say, "My parent(s) will tell other people they are proud of me, but that's for their own ego. Why won't they tell me?" Tell your children what you see as their strengths and accomplishments. Let them know that you respect them. Tell them you love them. Now tell them again.

You have a marvelous opportunity as a parent to break the cycle of negative events and experiences that sometimes go from generation to generation in families and were likely intensified by your parents' divorce and the experiences and beliefs that you then acquired. You will not always get it right, but relationships are rarely based on one event. Rather, you can build a history with your children of love, closeness, and respect that repeatedly demonstrates the importance to you of your child(ren) and your relationship(s). You can replicate the positive experiences you had with your parents and rewrite the script around the negative events to experience the joy of parenthood and give your children and grandchildren the gifts of your love. As one father who was a child of divorce himself said to us, "I want to give my children a different and better childhood than I had."

Conclusion

Your experience during and after your parents' divorce has not been without pain and other negative effects. It has been stressful and has contributed to how you see yourself and your relationships with others. Yet, it is just the experiences of one child in one family going through an incredibly stressful series of life events over a long period of time and for which most of the participants were ill-prepared. We hope that through reading this book and examining some of your own life events you can see yourself as a freestanding individual, able to love and be loved, able to be appropriately intimate and vulnerable in your relationships, and able to have healthy relationships with your parents, your significant others, and your own children.

Your parents' divorce was a milestone in your life but does not have to be the defining element of who you are. As an adult, you can define yourself and your relationships in healthy ways, acknowledging the pain while reaching for and appreciating the joys that life and your relationships offer.

References and Suggested Readings

References

Blau, M. 1993. *Families Apart: Ten Keys to Successful Co-Parenting.* New York: The Berkley Publishing Group.

Hetherington, E. M., and J. Kelly. 2002. *For Better or for Worse: Divorce Reconsidered.* New York: W. W. Norton & Company.

Kelly, J., and J. Johnston. 2001. A Reformulation of Parental Alienation Syndrome. *Family Court Review* 39:249-266.

Thayer, E., and J. Zimmerman. 2001. *The Co-Parenting Survival Guide: Letting Go of Conflict after a Difficult Divorce.* Oakland, CA.: New Harbinger Publications.

Wallerstein, J., J. Lewis, and J. Blakeslee. 2000. *The Unexpected Legacy of Divorce.* New York: Hyperion.

Willetts-Bloom, M., and S. Nock. 1992. The Effects of Childhood Family Structure and Perceptions of Parents' Marital Happiness on Familial Aspirations. In *Divorce and the Next Generation: Effects on Young Adults' Patterns of Intimacy and Expectations for Marriage.* New York: The Haworth Press, Inc.

Suggested Readings

Berner, R. T. 1992. *Parents Whose Parents Were Divorced.* New York: The Haworth Press.

Burns, B., and M. Brissett, Jr. 1991. *The Adult Child of Divorce: A Recovery Handbook.* Nashville: Thomas Nelson Publishers.

Conway, J. 1990. *Adult Children of Legal or Emotional Divorce: Healing Your Long-Term Hurt.* Downers Grove, IL: Intervarsity Press.

Hirschfeld, M. 1992. *The Adult Children of Divorce Workbook: A Compassionate Program for Healing from Your Parents' Divorce.* Los Angeles: Jeremy P. Tarcher, Inc.

Sandvig, K. 1990. *Adult Children of Divorce: Haunting Problems and Healthy Solutions.* Dallas: Word Publishing.

Staal, S. 2000. *The Love They Lost: Living with the Legacy of Our Parents' Divorce.* New York: Delacorte Press.

Jeffrey Zimmerman, Ph.D., is President and Cofounder of Beacon Behavioral Services, LLC (Avon, CT) and the P.E.A.C.E. Program (Parents Equally Allied to Co-parent Effectively), which is a specialized service for high-conflict divorced and divorcing parents. He is also a coauthor of *The Co-Parenting Survival Guide: Letting Go of Conflict after a Difficult Divorce.* Dr. Zimmerman is a member of the American Psychological Association and a member, Past President, and Fellow of the Connecticut Psychological Association. He is also a Diplomat and Founding Fellow of the American College of Advanced Practice Psychologists and is on the clinical faculty of the University of Connecticut Health Center.

Elizabeth S. Thayer, Ph.D., is a Vice President and Cofounder of Beacon Behavioral Services, LLC (Avon, CT) and the P.E.A.C.E. Program (Parents Equally Allied to Co-parent Effectively), which is a specialized service for high-conflict divorced and divorcing parents. She is also a coauthor of *The Co-Parenting Survival Guide: Letting Go of Conflict after a Difficult Divorce.* Dr. Thayer is a member of the American Psychological Association and Connecticut Psychological Association. She also serves on the State of Connecticut Board of Examiners in Psychology.

For more information on the P.E.A.C.E. program or on training opportunities for mental health professionals, contact Drs. Zimmerman and Thayer at

Beacon Behavioral Services, LLC
40 Dale Road, Suite 201
Avon, CT 06001
860-676-9350 (ext. 17)
jzimmerman@beaconbehavioral.com

Some Other
New Harbinger Titles

Helping Your Depressed Child, Item 3228 $14.95

The Couples's Guide to Love and Money, Item 3112 $18.95

50 Wonderful Ways to be a Single-Parent Family, Item 3082 $12.95

Caring for Your Grieving Child, Item 3066 $14.95

Helping Your Child Overcome an Eating Disorder, Item 3104 $16.95

Helping Your Angry Child, Item 3120 $17.95

The Stepparent's Survival Guide, Item 3058 $17.95

Drugs and Your Kid, Item 3015 $15.95

The Daughter-In-Law's Survival Guide, Item 2817 $12.95

Whose Life Is It Anyway?, Item 2892 $14.95

It Happened to Me, Item 2795 $17.95

Act it Out, Item 2906 $19.95

Parenting Your Older Adopted Child, Item 2841 $16.95

Boy Talk, Item 271X $14.95

Talking to Alzheimer's, Item 2701 $12.95

Helping a Child with Nonverbal Learning Disorder or Asperger's Syndrome, Item 2779 $14.95

The 50 Best Ways to Simplify Your Life, Item 2558 $11.95

When Anger Hurts Your Relationship, Item 2604 $13.95

The Couple's Survival Workbook, Item 254X $18.95

Loving Your Teenage Daughter, Item 2620 $14.95

The Hidden Feeling of Motherhood, Item 2485 $14.95

Parenting Well When You're Depressed, Item 2515 $17.95

Thinking Pregnant, Item 2302 $13.95

Call **toll free, 1-800-748-6273**, or log on to our online bookstore at **www.newharbinger.com** to order. Have your Visa or Mastercard number ready. Or send a check for the titles you want to New Harbinger Publications, Inc., 5674 Shattuck Ave., Oakland, CA 94609. Include $4.50 for the first book and 75¢ for each additional book, to cover shipping a̲n̲d̲ ̲h̲a̲n̲d̲l̲i̲n̲g̲.̲ ̲(̲C̲a̲l̲i̲f̲o̲r̲n̲i̲a̲ ̲r̲e̲s̲i̲d̲e̲n̲t̲s̲ please include appropriate sales t̲a̲x̲.̲)̲ ̲A̲l̲l̲o̲w̲ ̲t̲w̲o̲ ̲t̲o̲ ̲f̲i̲v̲e̲ weeks for delivery.

Prices subject to change without notice.

Adult children of divorce : how to overcome t
306.89 Z72a
69423
Zimmerman, Jeffrey